Horticulture

The Green World

Horticulture

Gail M. Lang, Ph.D.

Series Editor
William G. Hopkins
Professor Emeritus of Biology
University of Western Ontario

CHELSEA HOUSE
PUBLISHERS

An imprint of Infobase Publishing

Dedicated to my husband Jonathan, and to our parents Ron, Jane, and Annie who nurtured a love for things green and growing

Horticulture

Copyright © 2007 by Infobase Publishing

Chelsea House
An imprint of Infobase Publishing
132 West 31st Street
New York NY 10001

ISBN-10: 0-7910-8961-4
ISBN-13: 978-0-7910-8961-3

Library of Congress Cataloging-in-Publication Data

Lang, Gail M.
  Horticulture / Gail M. Lang.
     p. cm. — (The Green world)
  Includes bibliographical references and index.
  ISBN 0-7910-8961-4 (hardcover)
  1. Horticulture—Juvenile literature. I. Title. II. Series.

  SB102.L36 2006
  635—dc22   2006025585

Text and cover design by Keith Trego and Ben Peterson

Printed in the United States of America

Bang HP 10 9 8 7 6 5 4 3 2 1

This book is printed on acid-free paper.

Table of Contents

Introduction

By William G. Hopkins

"Have you thanked a green plant today?" reads a popular bumper sticker. Indeed, we should thank green plants for providing the food we eat, fiber for the clothing we wear, wood for building our houses, and the oxygen we breathe. Without plants, humans and other animals simply could not exist. Psychologists tell us that plants also provide a sense of well-being and peace of mind, which is why we preserve forested parks in our cities, surround our homes with gardens, and install plants and flowers in our homes and workplaces. Gifts of flowers are the most popular way to acknowledge weddings, funerals, and other events of passage. Gardening is one of the fastest-growing hobbies in North America and the production of ornamental plants contributes billions of dollars annually to the economy.

Human history has been strongly influenced by plants. The rise of agriculture in the Fertile Crescent of Mesopotamia brought previously scattered hunter-gatherers together into villages. Ever since, the availability of land and water for cultivating plants has been a major factor in determining the location of human settlements. World exploration and discovery was driven by the search for herbs and spices. The cultivation of New World crops—sugar,

vii

cotton, and tobacco—was responsible for the introduction of slavery to America, the human and social consequences of which are still with us. The push westward by English colonists into the rich lands of the Ohio River valley in the mid-1700s was driven by the need to increase corn production and was a factor in precipitating the French and Indian War. The Irish potato famine in 1847 set in motion a wave of migration, mostly to North America, that would reduce the population of Ireland by half over the next 50 years.

As a young university instructor directing biology tutorials in a classroom that looked out over a wooded area, I would ask each group of students to look out the window and tell me what they saw. More often than not, the question would be met with a blank, questioning look. Plants are so much a part of our environment and the fabric of our everyday lives that they rarely register in our conscious thought. Yet today, faced with disappearing rain forests, exploding population growth, urban sprawl, and concerns about climate change, the productive capacity of global agricultural and forestry ecosystems is put under increasing pressure. Understanding plants is even more essential as we attempt to build a sustainable environment for the future.

The Green World series opens doors to the world of plants. The series describes what plants are, what plants do, and where plants fit in the overall scheme of things. *Horticulture* shows us how humans have learned to cultivate plants for use as ornamentals and to produce fruits and vegetables. We also learn the impact of horticultural methods on the environment and the importance of developing sustainable methods for future food production and protection of the environment.

1 10,000 Years of Horticulture

Agriculture is not the result of a happening, an idea, an invention, discovery or instruction by a god or goddess. It is the result of long periods of intimate co-evolution between plants and man.

– Jack Harlan (1917–1998)
American geneticist and plant breeder

10,000 Years of Horticulture

The practice of horticulture has been around for thousands of years, but how is it relevant to life in the twenty-first century? Plants still represent an important source of food, fuel, clothing, shelter, medicine, perfume, and recreation; they also add oxygen to the atmosphere and help in the removal of toxic waste from the soil. We have become dependent on commercial horticulture to supply our produce and other plant products. What if your favorite fruits or vegetables were no longer commercially available? You would either have to **cultivate** the plants yourself or go without them. The act of cultivation could be as simple as the use of a hoe to weed and loosen the ground under a berry bush you found in the woods or as complicated as the design and maintenance of a year-round vegetable garden.

Horticulture is the scientific term for the act of gardening. It first came into use around the eighteenth century, though gardening itself has been practiced for many thousands of years. A gardener must prepare and maintain the soil, select plants based on the **climate** and purpose for the garden, protect plants from adverse weather conditions and pests, and encourage growth with water and nutrients when necessary. Other roles of the gardener may include the **propagation** and **breeding** of new plants. All of these topics will be described in greater detail throughout this book.

Forestry, agronomy, and horticulture make up three branches of agricultural science. Forestry is a discipline that concentrates on trees that grow in a forest. **Agronomy** focuses on cereal crops, such as oats, barley, and wheat plus the **forage** crops that feed domesticated animals in pastures. The word *horticulture* derives from the Latin word *hortus,* which was used in Roman times to define a garden on an estate—usually one smaller than five acres. Anything larger than this was referred to as a farm.

Horticulture can be divided into four areas of specialty, two of which are dedicated to the production of food. The branch of horticulture that specializes in the growth of vegetable crops is

Figure 1.1 A man inspects grapes in a Burgundy vineyard near Beaune, France. Viticulturalists, scientists who study the cultivation of grapes, plan and oversee the growing of grapes that are used to make wine.

called **olericulture,** whereas **pomology** is devoted to the art of fruit cultivation. Vegetables and small fruits such as strawberries are grown in gardens but may also be grown in large commercial fields. Fruits found on trees, such as apples, pears, and peaches, are cultivated in **orchards,** whereas citrus and olive trees are grown in **groves.** Grapes are produced in vineyards in a process called **viticulture** (Figure 1.1).

Cultivation of ornamental houseplants and flowering plants is the third branch of horticulture and is called **floriculture** when conducted on a commercial scale. The fourth branch, **landscape horticulture,** focuses on **woody ornamentals** (shrubs and trees), which are cultivated in **nurseries** for distribution to the public, as well as **turf** grasses used for lawns. Plants grown in orchards, vineyards, groves, gardens, greenhouses, and nurseries all belong in the realm of horticulture.

ORIGINS OF HORTICULTURE

The origins of horticulture are vague because the first acts of plant cultivation by humans predate historical records. **Archaeological data** indicate that the cultivation of plants on a large and detectable scale coincided with global climate changes approximately 10,000 years ago. The warmer, wetter weather that followed the end of the last ice age caused changes in sea level, increased edible plant diversity, and caused human migrations into new areas. This large-scale cultivation event is referred to as the **neolithic revolution.**

Cultivation of plants on a small scale may have been practiced for many thousands of years prior to this. The protection and encouragement of the growth of wild food plants through weeding, pruning, irrigation, and pest control, along with the simple propagation of seeds or **cuttings,** most likely constituted some of the first human horticulture. The use of fire to remove dead vegetation and promote the new growth of desirable plants is another example of how ancient humans engaged in plant cultivation.

Archaeological evidence suggests that cereal crops were **domesticated** first. Domesticated crops have genetic and **morphological** differences from their wild ancestors that make them better suited for human use. These differences were the result of natural mutations for characteristics such as a larger grain size in wheat, which was selected for over time because the early horticulturists planted only the larger seeds that contained the genetic sequences for these traits. Most of the domesticated, edible plants we cultivate today are descended from wild plants found in the Near East, China, Southeast Asia, and the Americas.

HORTICULTURAL METHODOLOGY

Over the years, humans have compiled an impressive compendium of horticultural techniques through trial and error. The earliest written records of horticultural practices are from the first millennium B.C. in China, Mesopotamia (now called Iraq), and Egypt, followed by Greece and Rome. Some of the practices mentioned in these ancient writings include the use of iron tools; manure applications; **crop rotation**; **double cropping**; large-scale **irrigation** projects; **pollination, pruning,** and **grafting** of fruit trees; pest and disease control; as well as the identification, classification, and use of plants. Many of these methods are still applied today. These texts also describe methods that may not have been in common use even in ancient times. Similarly, modern texts on cultural methods include some practices that are not widely used but that have been documented nonetheless.

Ancient Egyptians created formal gardens with pools, a spice and perfume industry, and collections of medicinal plants. Mesopotamia had irrigated **terraces**, gardens, and parks. Significant contributions to **taxonomy** and plant **physiology** were made by the Greeks. Romans fostered the development of ornamental horticulture with **topiary** gardens, and they also used rudimentary greenhouses made of **mica** to force vegetable production.

The majority of the popular edible plants we grow today were cultured by these ancient civilizations as well as those found in Central and South America. Many **cultivars** (**culti**vated **var**iety) were generated from wild plants by 2000 B.C. Since our ancestors had a remarkable knowledge of wild, edible food plants—likely unsurpassed by contemporary humans—it is probable that they succeeded in the cultivation of the majority of plants that can be used for this purpose. Comparatively few new food plants have been domesticated in recent times, although many new varieties or cultivars of the ancient plants have been bred since then.

CONVENTIONAL VERSUS ORGANIC PRODUCE

Conventional produce is grown using methods based on technology from the industrial revolution and the development of agricultural chemistry. Nineteenth-century scientists such as

Jean Baptiste Boussingault and Justus von Liebig demonstrated that plants obtain nutrients from minerals dissolved in water. This is the basis of **hydroponics** (Figure 1.2), a system where plants are grown without soil in a solution of minerals. Previously it was

Proposed Geographic Origins of Edible Domesticated Plants

Near East, Egypt, and the Mediterranean – apple, cherry, date, fig, grape, olive, pear, plum, cabbage, broccoli, cauliflower, caraway, leek, carrot, hazelnut, melon, garlic, lettuce, pea, onions, beet, chard, pistachio, almond, dill, parsley, poppy, lentil, carob, and flax

Mountains of Central and Western China – apricot, peach, cucumber, adzuki bean, water chestnut, wasabi horseradish, ginger, cinnamon, and bamboo

Southeast Asia and the Pacific Islands – grapefruit, orange, lemon, lime, tangerine, banana, mango, clove, nutmeg, black pepper, turmeric, cardamom, sugarcane, coconut, mung bean, taro, and eggplant

Central America – pepper, green bean, squash, pumpkin, sweet potato, sunflower, vanilla, corn, scarlet runner bean, lima bean, pineapple, guava, and jicama

South America – avocado, tomato, potato, chocolate, peanut, cashew, beans, squash, yam, and papaya

The relatively recent domestication of the sunflower, blueberry, strawberry, cranberry, and bramble fruits (raspberry and blackberry) were bred from wild plants of the eastern United States.

Source: Jack R. Harlan, *Crops & Man* (Madison, Wisc.: American Society of Agronomy, Crop Science Society of America, 1975).

Figure 1.2 In this photograph, farmers plant lettuce in a hydroponic channel system in a commercial greenhouse. Commercial hydroponic crop production is more expensive than traditional soil-based crop production, which is why it is less common.

believed that plants "ate" **humus** (also called **compost** or **organic matter**). Compost is the residue from decomposed organic matter derived from plants and animals. It is now widely believed that both minerals and compost contribute to the growth of healthy plants. Hydroponics methods are often used to produce commercial greenhouse crops and are described further in Chapter 6.

Conventional methods use chemical fertilizers in place of humus plus large quantities of pesticides to control insects, microbial diseases, and **weeds**. Heavy **tillage** (plowing of the soil) with oil-fueled machinery to reduce human labor and large fields planted with a single type of crop year after year, a practice referred to as **monocropping,** were also introduced. The main benefit to monocropping is that plants all grow at the same rate, have the same water and nutrient needs, and can be harvested at the same time. This helps to reach the goal of the conventional approach, which is to maximize both **yield** and profit.

Vegetables and fresh-cut flowers were traditionally grown in fields close to their markets; the growers had a wide variety of produce. Farm fields became less diverse with the advent of good road networks and refrigeration technologies that allowed for produce to be shipped to distant parts of the country. The increase in competition from regions with mild climates and long growing seasons caused other growers to specialize in crops that they could grow more economically in their area.

Although the use of conventional methods may initially result in higher yields than the old-fashioned methods, there are problems with regard to long-term use since it decreases soil fertility and causes water pollution. The drawbacks to this method were not immediately apparent, but we now know that over time the heavy use of chemical fertilizers and pesticides harms the **microbes** in the soil, which ultimately reduces yield by causing infertility. The microbes in the soil are directly related to the availability of nutrients for plant growth. Soil infertility leads to weak plants that are more susceptible to microbial

Figure 1.3 In McAllen, Texas, a plane sprays insecticide on a field of carrots. Although they have been credited for an increase in the agricultural production of the twentieth century, insecticides can be toxic to both humans and the environment.

pathogens or insect **infestation** and thus require the application of more pesticides.

Many pesticides contain chemicals that are toxic to wildlife and humans and that persist in the environment for years. Insecticides influence the evolution of the target insect, which becomes resistant to the chemical. This necessitates the continual introduction of new chemicals into the environment (Figure 1.3). Entry of these chemicals into the groundwater endangers our fresh drinking water supplies. Some insecticides can cause damage to the nervous system in humans.

Excessive amounts of fertilizer also enter into the groundwater and the surface water. Soluble chemical fertilizers have historically been added to the soil in amounts greater than the plants could immediately consume. Heavy rain or irrigation of the crops drains soluble fertilizer from the soil into the groundwater in a process called **leaching.** Many wells have been closed over the years because of excessive **nitrates** that were added to the soil as nitrogen fertilizer.

Excess nutrients such as nitrate or **phosphate** may also **run off** into the surface water because of soil **erosion** from heavy irrigation or rainfall events. This causes problems with excessive **algal growth,** which reduces habitat for fish. A region in the Gulf of Mexico is called the Dead Zone because it becomes overgrown with algae every summer as a result of nutrients that enter the Gulf from the Mississippi River. As the algae decompose, oxygen in the water is used up and the fish die. The Dead Zone is about the size of the state of Rhode Island.

An additional problem is the use of heavy equipment, which causes compaction of the soil and results in the loss of good **soil** structure necessary for plant growth. To avoid this problem and also to lessen the possibility of erosion, some growers decline to till the soil. Usually, they instead add large amounts of **herbicides** to kill weeds that would otherwise be dug up by tillage. Some herbicides have been reported to affect the reproductive system in animals.

ORGANIC PRODUCE

Organic produce is grown with the old-fashioned methods used prior to the Industrial Revolution in an effort to stop or reverse damage done to the environment. Over the years, these methods have been improved. Sir Howard Albert is known as the father of the organic movement, which is based on the use of compost. He developed the **Indore method** of composting, while working as a British agronomist in India from 1905 to 1934. The benefits of compost as compared with chemical fertilizers include improved soil structure, better ability to retain water, higher retention of nutrients in the soil, and the introduction of beneficial soil microbes that suppress pathogens and help plants obtain nutrients.

The nutrients are released more slowly from compost and are not leached as rapidly from the soil as are the highly soluble

Figure 1.4 Kitchen scraps have been added to the top of this compost pile and should be mixed into the center of the pile with a pitchfork or shovel. Mixing the pile provides for optimal decomposition and discourages animal scavengers. Composts are used to improve soil fertility and are made up of organic materials.

chemical fertilizers. Compost begins with plant residues and/or animal manures that are aged 3 to 6 months (Figure 1.4). Animal and plant residues that would otherwise contribute to the pollution of waterways and landfills are recycled into a low-cost fertilizer and soil amendment.

Biodynamic methods were introduced by Rudolph Steiner in the 1920s. Specialized compost recipes and soil amendments are used to develop beneficial soil microbes. Astrological conditions, such as phases of the moon, are used to determine when to sow seeds and **transplant**. This approach has a limited but dedicated following worldwide, as does another form of organic cultivation called permaculture, developed in Australia by Bill Mollison. Permaculture integrates the garden into the natural landscape.

J.I. Rodale edited the *Encyclopedia of Organic Gardening* in 1959 in response to the American public's request for an approach to the cultivation of produce free from chemical residues. The method has been popular with home gardeners ever since and has grown steadily in the commercial sector through the 1990s and into the 21st century. The common goal with all organic approaches is to grow high-quality produce while having only a low impact on the environment. The methods can also be applied in floriculture and landscape horticulture.

Companion plants and crop rotations are used to take advantage of natural interactions between plants, soil microbes, and insects and thus reduce the need for fertilizer and pesticides. High genomic diversity in crops is encouraged, as it reduces the chance of disease-induced crop failure and offers a greater selection of produce to the grower and consumer.

The organic approach requires more planning and can be more labor-intensive than the conventional approach; however, organic produce can be sold in the market for more money than conventional produce. Increased consumer demand for pesticide-free produce has resulted in a rise in the number of organic farms and increased the distribution from local farmers markets to organic produce sections in large supermarket chains.

In October 2002, the United States Department of Agriculture (USDA) adopted a set of regulations for the national certification of organic farms. Prior to this, certification was granted on a state-by-state or regional basis only. These regulations prohibit the sale of **genetically modified organisms** (GMOs) under the organic label but do allow for the chemical- and radiation-induced mutations used for plant breeding purposes. Additionally, the use of chemical fertilizers is prohibited and the use of organic pesticides is tightly regulated.

Organic pesticides are derived from plants and other natural sources. Since some organic pesticide substances may be toxic to humans and wildlife, they are used in small quantities and only as a last resort. The consumer may not know which pesticides were used and how soon prior to harvest they were applied; therefore it is advisable to always wash your produce thoroughly to remove potential pesticide residue.

SUSTAINABLE HORTICULTURE

Sustainable horticulture combines conventional and organic methods in an effort to transition conventional growers to a more ecologically sensitive approach. This approach uses knowledge of the nutrient requirements for specific stages of growth for each crop in order to apply supplemental fertilizers, water, and pest control measures only at the time and in the amounts needed for that stage of growth. **Integrated pest management (IPM)** strategies use **biological control** and crop rotation to reduce pesticide use.

In 1985, Congress set up the LISA (Low Input Sustainable Agriculture) program, which has since been renamed SARE (Sustainable Agriculture and Research Education). In 1991, SARE and the EPA (Environmental Protection Agency) launched a joint venture to reduce agricultural pollution. Although sustainable methods are promoted by the U.S. government and **land-grant colleges** with extensive research in the field, they have yet to be adopted by the majority of growers in the United States because of the fear that reliance on organic methods will reduce yield and be incompatible with socioeconomic needs.

SUMMARY

This chapter introduced you to the 10,000-year history of horticulture, the geographical origins of domesticated, edible food plants, and the methodologies used to grow them. The general principles and philosophies of the different methods used in the conventional, organic, and sustainable approaches to growing were also described. The chapters that follow will acquaint you in more detail with the skills required of a horticulturist and present some options for the professional application of these skills.

If you do not know the names of things the knowledge is lost.

—Carolus Linnaeus (1707–1778)
Swedish botanist

Classification of Plants

Can you imagine how confusing life would be if we had no names and every time you wanted to refer to a person, place, or thing you had to describe it and its relationship to all others of its kind? We are fortunate that our predecessors came up with the idea of names and that knowledge about plants has been successfully passed down from generation to generation.

Classification is a term used to describe the process of grouping related plants together and naming the groups. These groups have been historically based on morphological and anatomical features and, more recently, on genetics. Members of a species have characteristics that set them apart from all other populations of plants, and they naturally breed with each other. Closely related species with similar characteristics are grouped into a genus. The genera are grouped into families and the families are grouped into classes. All the land plant classes collectively form two divisions, the bryophytes and the tracheophytes.

Bryophytes are called nonvascular plants because they have a very poorly developed **vascular system.** Since the vascular system is involved in the transport of water throughout the plant, bryophytes are generally—but not always—found in moist places and go **dormant** when water is scarce. There are approximately 24,000 species of bryophytes, most of which are mosses. These plants are not widely cultivated commercially but may be of great interest to botanists and naturalists. Mosses may sometimes be found growing on moist surfaces in greenhouses.

Tracheophytes have a well-developed vascular system that enables them to grow taller than bryophytes and to survive temporary shortages of water. They are divided into seed plants and seedless plants. The seedless plants reproduce by **spores** and many are found in wet habitats. Ferns are seedless tracheophytes that are sometimes grown in gardens or as houseplants.

Tracheophytes that produce seeds are divided into two groups, the gymnosperms and the angiosperms. Gymnosperms are plants that produce seeds that are not enclosed in an **ovary,** such as the cycads, gingko, conifers, and gnetinae. The cycads have palm or fern-like leaves and produce cones. Gingko trees have broad, **deciduous** leaves and stinky, fleshy fruits. Conifers such as the *Pinus spp.* (pines) and *Picea spp.* (spruce) have needle-like **evergreen** leaves and produce seeds in cones, whereas *Juniperus spp.* (junipers) may have scale-like leaves and produce their seeds in berries. The gnetinae, which include *Ephedra spp.*, have **xylem** vessels similar to those found in mosses, horsetails, and ferns. Of all the gymnosperms, the conifers are the most widely cultivated. Gingko trees are also often used for landscaping, especially along roads and in public places.

Angiosperms are seed plants that produce flowers. The seeds are enclosed in a mature ovary, which forms a fruit. There are more than 250,000 species of angiosperms; this group is the most widely cultivated group of plants on Earth. Angiosperms are divided into two classes, the monocots and the dicots, based on **morphology** and anatomy. Monocots have seeds with a single **cotyledon**; dicot seeds have two cotyledons. These traits are the basis for these groups' names: *monocot* is short for "monocotyledon" (*mono-* means "single") and *dicot* is short for "dicotyledon" (*di-* means "two"). The parts of monocot flowers (**sepals, petals, stamens,** ovary) usually occur in multiples of three, whereas the parts of dicot flowers are found in multiples of four or five. Additionally, monocot leaves have parallel venation. Dicot leaves have net venation because of the arrangement of their vascular system. Figures 2.1 and 2.2 show some of the differences between monocot and dicot plant parts.

The vascular system is a transportation network of connected cells that form tunnels in the plant that extend from the roots through the stem to the leaves, flowers, and fruits. Xylem transports water and minerals upwards from the roots and distributes it throughout the plant. **Phloem** transports the sugars created by **photosynthesis** from the leaves to other parts of the plant. These tunnels are bundled together and can be seen as the veins on a leaf.

Figure 2.1 (TOP) The lily is an example of a monocot with flower parts typically found in multiples of three. There are three outer sepals, which in this example look identical to the three inner petals. The stigma has three lobes and there are six stamens. Florists will often remove the anthers from the stamens because they shed large amounts of pollen. (BOTTOM) The veins of leaves of monocots, such as this lily leaf, run parallel to each other.

Figure 2.2 (TOP) The hibiscus flower is a dicot with five petals, five small green sepals, a five-lobed stigma, and many yellow stamens fused to the style. (BOTTOM) This hybrid camellia is a dicot with a rose-like flower. The veins of leaves of dicots form a net-like pattern, known as net venation.

The monocot and dicot classes are subdivided further into families. Members of botanical families share similar characteristics. For example, plants in the Lamiaceae family have characteristically square stems, and many have **trichome hairs**. These hairs can make the leaves or stems feel rough, and they help reduce airflow across the surface of the leaf. Glandular trichome hair secretes **essential oils** and **resins,** which can make these surfaces sticky or fragrant. Many medicinal and culinary herbs, such as mint, sage, lavender, and thyme, are grown for their ability to produce essential oils and resins.

Plants in the family Solanaceae produce mildly to highly poisonous **alkaloids** and have similar flowers. The introduction of tomato and potato crops from the Americas to Europe took some time because of the reputation of their highly toxic relatives, such as the deadly nightshade.

Plants in the family **Leguminosae** also have similar flowers and produce fruits called legumes. The pea flower and pea pods are examples of Leguminosae flowers and fruits. Many of these plants also have important relationships with soil bacteria that are capable of **nitrogen fixation**. The bacteria form **nodules** in the roots of the plants.

Seed catalogs, plant encyclopedias, and garden centers often group plants in ways other than by family—for example, by life cycle, edibility, cultural requirements, or geography. Life cycle can be annual, biennial, or perennial. Annual plants flower and set seed in the first year and then die. They generally bloom all summer but need to be replanted every year; sometimes they will self-sow if the flowers have been allowed to go to seed. Biennials flower and produce seed in the second year and then die. Perennials take two or more years to flower and set seed, and they live for many years. They generally bloom every year after the first flower. Perennials usually bloom for a short period each season and then die back until the following spring. They can be short-lived (four to five years) or long-lived (many thousands of years) like the bristlecone and Sequoia pine trees.

The Wide World of Angiosperms

There are approximately 250,000 known species of angiosperms. The table below lists angiosperm plants divided into the dicot and monocot classes and further divided into families and genus. The binomial nomenclature is in italics and the common name is in parentheses. The approximate number of species is listed after the common name. Each species may have numerous cultivars (the daylily has over 30,000) that are developed for specific traits and adapted to different growing conditions. Some cultivars improve crop yield and others are grown because of their unique appearance or taste.

DICOT PLANTS
Lamiaceae
Lavendula spp. (lavender) 25
Mentha spp. (mint) 25
Salvia spp. (sage) 900
Thymus spp. (thyme) 350

Leguminosae
Glycine max (soybean)
Medicago sativa (alfalfa)
Phaseolus vulgaris (common bean)
Pisum sativum (garden pea)

Rosaceae
Fragaria spp. (strawberry) 12
Malus spp. (apple) 35
Prunus spp. (plum, peach, cherry, almond) 200
Pyrus spp. (pear) 30
Rubus spp. (raspberry, blackberry) 250

Solanaceae
Capsicum annuum (chili, sweet pepper)
Lycopersicum esculentum (tomato)
Solanum tuberosum (potato)

MONOCOT PLANTS
Amaryllidaceae
Allium cepa (onion)
A. sativum (garlic)
Narcissus spp. (daffodil) 50

Liliaceae
Hemerocallis spp. (daylily) 15
Lilium spp. (lily) 100
Tulipa spp. (tulip) 100

Poaceae
Festuca spp. (fescue) 400
Poa spp. (bluegrass) 500
Zea mays (sweet corn)

Source: Christopher Brickell and Judith D. Zuk, *The American Horticultural Society A–Z Encyclopedia of Garden Plants* (New York: DK Publishing, 1996).

Deciduous plants lose their leaves in the fall, whereas ever-green plants retain their leaves year round. Some deciduous plants have brilliant displays of colorful foliage in the fall prior to leaf drop. This is due to the **carotinoid** pigments, which are colored in shades of red and yellow. The green **chlorophyll** pigments are more numerous when the plant is growing, so during this time carotinoid pigments are masked by the green. When the plant gets ready to go dormant, it stops producing chlorophyll and the red and yellow pigments become visible.

Cultural requirements include the amount of sun and water required by plants, the preferred temperature and soil type, and nutrient needs as described in Chapter 4. **Xeric** plants survive periods of drought; they are adapted to hot, dry summers and cool, moist winters. Shade plants, as you may have guessed, like to be shaded from the summer sun. Vegetables are often separated into warm-season and cool-season crops based on the temperatures at which their seeds prefer to germinate. Grasses are also classified as warm or cool season. Annual flowers are sometimes labeled as frost tolerant or frost sensitive.

Native plants are those that are believed to have originated in the region where they are to be cultivated. Generally, the cultivation of native plants requires less work because they are already adapted to the soil and climate. Plants may also be grouped according to the ecosystem where they are found growing wild, such as alpine, tropical, desert, or riparian. Alpine plants are found at high altitudes, tropical plants in rain forests, and riparian plants by rivers and streams.

PLANT NAMES

Many plants have been given common names. These tend to be locally derived, so multiple names may exist for a single plant species if it grows naturally in different parts of the world. There are also instances where the same common name is used for different plants. Thyme is the common name used for more than 350 species in the genus *Thymus*. Only a few of these species are used for culinary purposes, so it is important to purchase the correct plant if you want to eat it.

Horticulturists use a system of binomial nomenclature and cultivar names to identify a specific plant and thus avoid the confusion that can be caused by common names. Binomial nomenclature is a system that assigns a unique two-word name to each

What Exactly Is a Fruit?

Some foods we commonly think of as vegetables, such as the tomato or pea pod, are actually, botanically speaking, fruits. Peppers, squash, eggplant, cucumber, and sweet corn are also technically fruits. Fruits are formed after fertilization as the ovary ripens; while it develops, the other flower parts wither and die. The wall of the ovary becomes the pericarp (the outer layer of the fruit) and the fertilized ovules turn into seeds. Fruits can be fleshy or dry.

FLESHY FRUITS

The drupes (olive, plum, cherry) develop from a single ovary with a single ovule that becomes the pit. Pome fruits (apple, pear) grow from a compound ovary with many ovules and have distinct chambers with many seeds. Berries (tomato, pepper, grape) also have many seeds. Pepo fruits (melon, pumpkin, squash, cucumber) are fleshy with many seeds and a hard rind. Raspberries, strawberries, and blackberries are fleshy aggregate fruits that form from the fusion of many flowers. Parthenocarpic fruits do not develop seeds and can occur naturally (banana) or be chemically induced (oranges, watermelon).

DRY FRUITS

Dry fruits that break open to free the seeds while still attached to the plant are described as dehiscent. Some examples are legumes (pea pod), which develop from a single ovary that splits down both sides and capsules that grow from a compound ovary and open at the top (poppy). The pericarp of indehiscent fruits remains closed until after it falls off the plant; examples of these types of fruits are corn and nuts.

species, made up of a generic name (the genus) plus a specific name that defines the species. It was developed by Carolus Linnaeus in the eighteenth century (Figure 2.3). Linnaeus built upon the work of many prior botanists. The earliest records made by the fathers of botany date from the fifth century B.C. to the third century A.D. and recount knowledge from Mesopotamia, Egypt, Greece, and Rome. Arab and Asiatic botanical records from the eighth to the twelfth century A.D. and the work of botanists from the 1500s to the 1700s were also described by Linnaeus.

Binomial nomenclature was created in Latin, as this was a language common to botanists from different countries. The genus name is a Latin noun that may be the name of a person who discovered the plant or it may somehow describe a common trait of all the plants in the genus. The species name is a Latin adjective that modifies the noun based on a particular characteristic of the species, such as the color of the flowers or size of the plant. The genus is always capitalized; the species name is in lowercase and the full name is either italicized or underlined. (For example, the binomial name for corn is *Zea mays*.) The genus can be abbreviated by the first letter followed by a period in instances where it has been previously referred to in a manuscript. Sometimes the specific epithet is designated as *sp.* or *spp.* (plural) in cases where it is either not known or if the writer wants to refer to all plants in the genus.

The binomial nomenclature, or Latin name, may be modified to reflect a botanical variety or a horticultural cultivar that is noticeably different from other plants of the same species (though all members of a species—including the unique varieties and cultivars—can interbreed). The modification accounts for differences that occur in plants because of growth in various types of soil or spontaneous mutations that may produce a different color flower or **variegated** leaves, among other traits.

Varieties are plant specimens identified in their natural environment, whereas cultivars are those that were cultivated and bred by man. However, many subspecies of vegetables are called

Figure 2.3 Carolus Linnaeus was a Swedish botanist and taxonomist, referred to as the father of modern taxonomy. In 1749, Linnaeus laid the foundation for the classification of living organisms when he introduced binomial nomenclature.

varieties and the two terms are often used interchangeably. The cultivar or variety name is set in single quotes, is not italicized, and is limited to three words. The cultivar name either follows the binominal or is used in place of the species name. Collections of cultivars may be combined into larger horticultural groups.

Examples of Latin names, followed in parentheses by the common name(s), for the culinary species of thyme include *Thymus vulgaris* (common thyme, garden thyme), *T. herba-barona* (caraway thyme, herb baron) and *Thymus × citriodorus* (lemon-scented thyme). The × in *T. × citriodous* is used to designate it as a hybrid. Hybrids are a result of cross-breeding as described in the next chapter. *T. serpyllum* 'Coccineus' (red creeping thyme) is not an edible plant but is appropriate for use in a garden path or rock garden because of its creeping habit and colorful flowers. The word 'Coccineus' set in single quotation marks indicates that it is a cultivar name.

Plants need to be described before they can be identified. Plant anatomical and morphological characteristics are used to generate descriptions of plants and to group them according to their similarities in order to identify and name them. The best times to describe plants are when they are in full flower. Alternately, fruiting structures will yield a great deal of information. The order of the description follows the growth of the plant. It begins with the roots, moves to the stem and leaves, and ends with a description of the reproductive structures (flowers and fruits).

Once these features have been noted, one can consult a botanical text with a dichotomous key, field guides, illustrated encyclopedias, seed and plant catalogs, garden centers, botanical gardens, and herbariums for descriptions of similar plants that have been previously identified and named. A dichotomous key consists of paired statements that describe the characteristics of a plant. One of the statements will apply to the plant and directs the user to another set of paired statements. This continues until the plant is named. Pictures, illustrations, or dried specimens can be very helpful in the identification of plants.

Dried specimens are made by pressing the whole plant between sheets of paper, then mounting with glue. Herbariums are collections of pressed, dried plants that have been identified by botanists and can be found in botanical gardens, at universities, and in private collections (Figure 2.4). Dried specimens can

Figure 2.4 Botanists are photographed in Guyana as they identify and catalog plant specimens for an herbarium. An herbarium is a collection of preserved plant specimens.

be brought to an herbarium for identification by comparison to other plants in the collection.

SUMMARY

This chapter presented a classification of horticultural plants according to division, class, family, genus, and species, with an emphasis on the angiosperms—the most widely cultivated group of plants—and described the binominal nomenclature method for naming plants. Other popular methods for grouping plants were also presented. It is important to know how plants are related to one another and the environments where they are naturally found, as this generally helps in understanding their cultural requirements and in determining which plants should be grown together. Plants of the same species will interbreed. Plant propagation and breeding are the topics of Chapter 3.

3 Propagation and Breeding

*Animals are not essential; plants supply over 90%
of the food consumed by humans.*
—Jack Harlan, *The Living Fields* (1995)

Seed formation is initiated by changes in environmental conditions, such as the difference in daytime and nighttime temperatures and the relative number of hours of daylight versus darkness, and also by the production of plant hormones. The process begins with the development of flower buds. Pollination occurs after the flower blooms and involves the deposition of the male pollen onto the female stigma. Pollination is followed by fertilization, which is required to produce **viable** seeds. Fertilization occurs when sperm cells from the pollen grain reach the ovules in the ovary and combine with an egg. The fertilized egg develops into a seed that contains an embryonic plant in a dormant state. Reproductive structures are illustrated in Figure 3.1.

PROPAGATION OF NEW PLANTS FROM SEEDS

Seeds are dormant, embryonic plants developed from fertilized ovules. All seeds contain an embryonic stem, an embryonic root, and meristems. The seed is surrounded by a protective seed coat. In addition, monocot plants have a single large nutritious cotyledon, whereas dicots have two nutritious cotyledons. The cotyledons supply food to the seedling until it begins photosynthesis.

The most important factors for seed germination are a properly prepared seedbed, consistent moisture, and adequate temperature. Seeds from different plants have a wide range of temperatures and moisture conditions required to break dormancy. Dormancy occurs to protect the plant embryo from emergence under adverse conditions that could kill it while it is still young. The conditions can be quite specific and are provided with the seeds when they are purchased.

Temperature requirements range significantly; some plants require **vernalization**, whereas some will not germinate unless they have been involved in a fire, such as the seeds of the Ponderosa pine. Plants that require vernalization must be exposed to cold

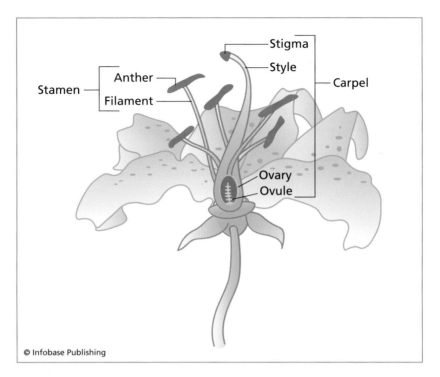

Figure 3.1 The female reproductive organ is called the carpel. The carpel is made up of a stigma and ovary connected by the style. The male reproductive organ is a stamen. The stamen consists of anthers, which contain the pollen grains, suspended on a thin filament. Pollen grains land on the stigma, which has a sticky surface, and develop a pollen tube that grows downward through the style until it reaches the ovary. The ovary contains ovules (eggs), and the pollen grains produce sperm. The sperm cells travel down the pollen tube and fertilize the ovules. The ovary grows into a fruit and the other parts wither away.

or freezing temperatures for a set length of time, followed by exposure to warm temperature. This happens naturally as the season progresses from winter to spring.

Pretreatments may be applied. Seeds are sometimes boiled in water to kill viruses or treated with pesticides to inhibit diseases that would kill the seedling. Seeds that need cold treatment can be put in a cooler or freezer or planted in potting soil and put outside over the winter. They can also be sown in the ground after the first frost so they will germinate in the spring.

Seeds of cool-season plants, such as peas and carrots, can be planted outdoors early in the spring. Warm-season plants like tomatoes and peppers are more sensitive to lower temperatures and can be started indoors (in a house, greenhouse, hotbed, or cold frame) and transplanted into the garden after the **last average frost date**. Cool-season vegetables are characterized as **hardy**

Specialized Flowers and Pollination

Pollination occurs in several different ways, depending on the structure of the flower:

Plants that self-pollinate are called selfers. For example, the reproductive structures of pea flowers are enclosed between two fused petals, called a keel, which ensures that self-fertilization takes place.

Wind-pollinated plants, such as trees and grasses, generally produce large amounts of small, light pollen that is not sticky. The flowers are not usually colorful, do not produce nectar, and have no odor. The flowers form before the leaves do and the stamens and stigmas are exposed to the wind. When these flowers are blown about by the wind, the pollen shakes loose from the anther of one plant and is deposited on the stigma of another plant. Most pollen can be carried up to 330 feet (100 meters) from the plant. These types of flowers are usually found in temperate regions and are rare in the tropics.

Insect pollinators pick up pollen grains as they feed on nectar from one plant and deposit it on subsequent plants that they visit. The flowers pollinated by insects tend to have sticky pollen that adheres to the hairs on the legs of the insects. There are approximately 20,000 species of bees attracted to sweet-scented flowers that produce nectar and 16 families of beetles that are lured to flowers with fruity, spicy, or pungent odors. Flies

or **half-hardy** and warm-season vegetables as **tender** or **very tender** based on their ability to tolerate frost.

Frost occurs when the temperature drops to freezing ($32°F$) or below and is visible as a white substance that needs to be scraped off of car windshields in the morning. It is frozen water vapor and can damage sensitive leaves. Frost pockets are regions where cool air settles, such as at the bottom of a hill, and are prone to frost earlier and later in the season then other areas. You can find

Figure 3.2 A butterfly uses its proboscis to suck nectar from a thyme flower.

also pollinate flowers as they feed. Butterflies have a long, thin proboscis to suck nectar from tubular flowers or flowers with a long style, but the pollen tends not to stick to their bodies and so they are not efficient pollinators (Figure 3.2).

out your last average frost date from the United States National Arboretum Web site listed in the Further Reading section of the book. Your local cooperative extension (described in Chapter 8) or a local garden center can also provide this information.

Seeds that are sown directly in the garden will need to be watered daily for at least several weeks unless there is sufficient rainfall to keep the ground moist. The seeds only need to be kept moist; heavy rainfall or irrigation may wash them away.

Seeds that are started indoors are planted in germination media in small pots or **flats** and provided with supplemental heat and light during late winter and early spring. Germination media is formulated from materials that absorb water and stay moist, such as peat moss, which is found in bogs and harvested for sale at nurseries. Some people are opposed to the harvest of peat moss because it takes a long time to grow in the wild, and will use other substances such as coir from coconuts or a well-ripened compost that has been passed through a fine-mesh screen.

Germination media may not provide many nutrients because it is assumed that the seedlings will be transplanted into a more nutritious soil or potting mix shortly after germination. If the pots or flats are placed inside a plastic bag or covered with glass, the plants remain moist and will not need to be misted. The plastic or glass creates a miniature greenhouse and retains the moisture from presoaked germination media. Commercial growers have dedicated germination rooms that supply the necessary heat and humidity and also supplemental light for seedlings that have developed their first true leaves and have started photosynthesizing.

PROPAGATION FROM CUTTINGS
Plants produced from cuttings will be clones of the parent plant. *Clone* is the Greek word for "twig" and describes plants that are reproduced without the benefit of sexual

Figure 3.3 Stem cuttings from a woody ornamental (Pyracantha) that have developed adventitious roots. Cuttings taken from the same plant will be genetically identical to the parent and to each other.

recombination; therefore, the genome of the offspring is identical to the parent. Cuttings can be taken from the stem, leaves, or roots. Stem or shoot cuttings are commonly used for the propagation of houseplants, cut flowers, woody ornamentals, and orchard trees (Figure 3.3).

A cut is made just above the node, which is the junction of a stem and leaf. A callus will form at the point of the cut and **adventitious roots** will grow from the stem. Some species will more readily form roots from cuttings than others. The process can be accelerated by the application of root hormones. Cuttings can also be taken from stem modifications, such as tubers. Most familiar is the potato, which sprouts from the eyes on a tuber. The tubers are cut into pieces so that each piece contains an eye; these are used as seed plants. Plants that form bulbous stems, such as onions and tulips, produce multiple bulblets that are dug up, divided, and transplanted.

Stolons, found on strawberry plants, are aboveground stem modifications with nodes that generate adventitious roots and shoots when they come into contact with the soil and can be used to generate new plants. Rhizomes are modified underground stems; some are edible (for example, ginger). Those found on the iris and many grass plants are not edible. Weeds that reproduce with rhizomes may become **invasive** and difficult to control because if the entire rhizome is not removed the plant will regenerate itself.

Grafting is a method that involves the combination of the rootstock from one plant to the scion (stem cutting) of a second. The rootstock is usually from plants that have been well established in the orchard or vineyard. They may have excellent disease resistance or some other characteristic that makes them vigorous growers. The rootstock includes the roots and the lower portion of the stem. The scion is from a plant that produces a fruit with a new trait that the grower wants to reproduce. In a successful graft, the vascular systems will combine and the scion will grow and set fruit on the host's rootstock. This procedure is often used with apple trees and grapevines.

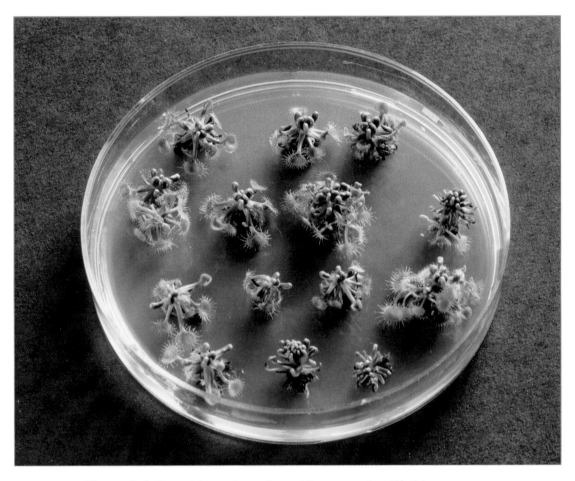

Figure 3.4 Round-leaved sundews (*Drosera rotundifolia*) are grown from tissue cultures on a gelatin media in a petri dish. In this process, known as micropropagation, clones are grown from single cells of a callus that formed from a wound inflicted on the parent plant.

TISSUE CULTURE

Some ornamental plants, including orchids and most transgenic crops, are reproduced by tissue culture (Figure 3.4). This involves the infliction of a wound to the parent plant so that it forms a callus from parenchyma cells. Parenchyma cells are most similar to meristem cells and represent up to 80% of all the cells in the plant. Meristem cells have a large nucleus and can repeatedly divide to produce daughter cells. Meristem cells are the plant equivalent of animal stem cells and are found in the meristem region at the tips of roots and shoots and in seeds. It is only when meristem cells migrate out of the meristem region that they differentiate into specialized cells that make up the rest of the plant. Once a meristem cell differentiates, it generally will not divide again, but parenchyma cells can divide in response to a wound and produce a callus, which is a mass of undifferentiated cells. These undifferentiated cells from the callus can be induced to differentiate into the specialized cells that will produce a full-grown plant.

The callus will generate a **somatic embryo** when grown on a nutritious gelatinous media supplemented with hormones. First, the callus is placed in a receptacle called a petri dish that contains a mix of chemical nutrients, high concentrations of cytokinin, and low concentrations of auxin, all of which have been solidified with gelatin. This ratio of high cytokinin to low auxin promotes shoot growth. After the shoots are formed, the **plantlets** are transferred to a second petri dish with a high auxin to low cytokinin ratio, which induces root growth. After root generation, they are transferred to potting soil.

TRANSPLANTING

Transplanting is simply the transfer of a seedling or young plant from one container to another or into the ground. Some plants, such as those that form taproots, would rather not be transplanted and should be sown where they are to grow. Taproots are enlarged primary roots that are sometimes used for food storage. Carrots and parsnips are examples of swollen taproots. Some horticulturists believe that multiple transplants into nutritious potting media or soil will benefit the plant and give higher yields.

Others think that transplanting causes shock to the plant and will cause it to be less vigorous. Both of these viewpoints are correct when taken in the proper context.

Whether seeds are sown directly in the ground where they will grow or are transplanted from container to container depends upon the type of roots formed by the plant and its cultural requirements, as well as the type of soil and climate. Roots can be damaged in the process and may have trouble accessing nutrients, especially if the soil bed has not been properly prepared. Phosphorous fertilizer is often applied, as it is the most difficult nutrient for damaged roots to access and it promotes development of new roots.

PLANT BREEDING

Crops that rely on wind or insect pollination but are grown in a greenhouse may have to be pollinated by hand. Cultivated plants may be hand-pollinated with a small paintbrush. The horticulturist brushes the anther of the stamen to retrieve pollen grains and then deposits them on the stigma of the female flower on another plant. Hand pollination is also used to cross-pollinate plants to create new hybrids. Plants that belong to the same species, including all the subspecies (varieties or cultivars), will naturally interbreed with each other to form hybrids. The approach to classification developed by Linnaeus, described in the previous chapter, gave insight into the relationship between speciation and plant breeding that was developed further by the work of Charles Darwin in the 1800s.

Luther Burbank was a prolific plant breeder who was inspired by a book written by Darwin in 1868 called *The Variation of Animals and Plants Under Domestication*. Burbank bred hundreds of new cultivars; the first of these was the Russet (or Burbank) potato in 1873. He then imported berries, plums, and nuts to

California and experimented with wide crosses between domestic and foreign cultivars. Wide crosses do not naturally occur and have unpredictable results that often cause mutations that are harmful to the plant. Therefore, this method involves the propagation and screening of millions of plants to find one healthy cultivar with a desirable new trait.

Chemical- and radiation-induced mutations were introduced in the 1900s. The plant is exposed to certain chemicals, X-rays, or gamma radiation, and this treatment produces unpredictable mutations to the target plant. When the mutation occurs in a somatic (nonreproductive) cell, the mutation may affect the plant itself but not the offspring unless the somatic cells are used to clone new plants. When it occurs in a germ cell (sperm or egg), the mutation is passed to the offspring. Most of these mutations are not beneficial to the plant or to humans so this method also requires the propagation and screening of millions of plants to establish a useful new cultivar. Rio red grapefruit and wheat are commercial crops with radiation-induced mutations. A chemically mutated barley cultivar, introduced in 1995, is widely used in beer and a mutated commercial peanut cultivar was bred in 1959.

Transgenic plants are plants that have had genes from an unrelated organism inserted into the chromosome by **genetic engineering** for the purpose of breeding a new cultivar (Figure 3.5). Sources of these genes include other plants, microbes, and fish. The genes that have been used to transform plants code for traits such as resistance to specific microbial infections, resistance to cold temperatures, resistance to drought and salt, **parthenocarpy**, resistance to herbicides, and the creation of pesticides.

The most controversial transgenic plants are those that create pesticides. Government regulatory agencies classify the gene product as a pesticide and not a food additive; therefore, the FDA

Figure 3.5 Genetically engineered crops, or products involved in ongoing or planned transgenic studies, are photographed above. Genetic engineering, the process of manipulating genes, remains a controversial issue around the world.

(Food and Drug Administration) is not involved in the establishment of safety guidelines for pesticide residue in transformed crops.

Biologists cannot control where on the chromosome the integration of the inserted gene occurs, and the process will most likely cause a problem by interfering with the function of other important genes. Because of this, genetic engineering offers no time- or labor-saving advantage over wide crosses and chemical- or radiated-induced mutations, as this process also requires the propagation and screening of millions of plants to come up with a healthy new cultivar.

The unpredictable results obtained from wide crosses, chemical- and radiation-induced mutations, and genetic engineering may be a result of transposable elements. Transposable elements are naturally occurring, mobile segments of DNA (deoxyribonucleic acid). They play an important role in genetic engineering. Transposable elements can cause a whole segment of chromosome to be duplicated, moved to another chromosome, or even deleted. The genome can be radically altered and the result is offspring that are different from both parents. Transposable elements are found in all genomes that have been studied to date and are inhibited by naturally occurring modifications to the DNA. These modifications may be inherited and prevent the activity of the transposable element. Transposable elements can be triggered by X-rays, gamma rays, wide crosses, and tissue culture techniques, which explains the unpredictable results of breeding methods.

It has been suggested that a rise in the number of people susceptible to food allergies may be attributed to the introduction of new cultivars bred with methods that can trigger transposable elements. Peanuts, wheat, soy, and barley are examples of crops that may have acquired subtle mutations that trigger allergies. Extensive research would be required to confirm whether this is the case.

SUMMARY

This chapter provided an introduction to the methods involved in plant breeding and propagation. The breeding of plants that are resistant to disease is very important, as it helps to reduce the amount of pesticides that must be applied. It was shown that regardless of the method used for breeding, millions of plants must be propagated before a useful cultivar can be established. This illustrates why the science of horticulture took many thousands of years to establish.

4 Cultural Requirements

Not every soil can bear all things.
–Virgil (70 B.C.–19 B.C.)
Ancient Roman poet

Cultural Requirements

If you only ate one meal a week, do you think you would grow as tall as you would otherwise? How long could you last without water or air? We all have basic requirements necessary to maintain a healthy body. These include oxygen, water, carbohydrates, and other nutrients. Plants are no different. They require these things as well, and it is the job of the horticulturist to make sure that they get them.

We get our oxygen from the atmosphere. So do plants, but it must first diffuse into the soil because they respire or "breathe" with their roots. For this reason, there must be a balance of air and water in the soil. Many plants die from overwatering because they do not get enough oxygen. On the other hand, if the plant does not receive enough water, it wilts and eventually dies because it accesses nutrients from minerals dissolved in the water and because water is necessary for photosynthesis.

We get carbohydrates from eating plants. Plants, however, make their own carbohydrates with photosynthesis. Photosynthesis runs on solar energy, which is used to combine carbon dioxide and water into the sugar called glucose. It happens in the green-pigmented **chloroplasts** found in the parenchyma cells of leaves (Figure 4.1).

The duration and intensity of sunshine; the quality of the soil; and such environmental factors as temperature, annual rainfall, humidity, and wind are all variables that affect plant growth. As you may have noticed, not everyone requires the same amount of food or water. Also, some of us actually like cold weather, whereas others prefer the heat. The specific cultural requirements of a plant in a vegetable garden are different from those of a plant in the wildflower meadow, as are those that evolved in alpine versus tropical versus desert environments. Cultural requirements for sunshine, soil quality, water, and climate are described below.

SUNSHINE

Plants have specific requirements for light intensity, quality, and night length. Light intensity refers to the strength of the sunlight.

48

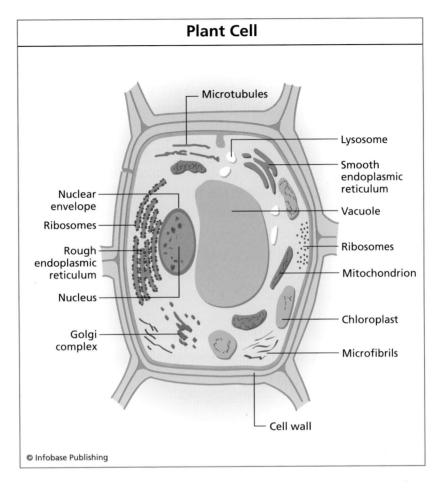

Plant Cell

Microtubules

Lysosome

Smooth endoplasmic reticulum

Nuclear envelope

Vacuole

Ribosomes

Rough endoplasmic reticulum

Ribosomes

Mitochondrion

Nucleus

Golgi complex

Chloroplast

Microfibrils

Cell wall

© Infobase Publishing

Figure 4.1 A plant cell consists of numerous specialized organelles. Photosynthesis occurs within the chloroplast. Other organelles include ribosomes, mitochondrion, smooth and rough endoplasmic reticulum, and the nucleus, which contains the plant cell's DNA.

The optimum intensity for plant growth is that at which the plant is most proficient at photosynthesis. Higher than optimum light intensity can damage chloroplasts, whereas lower levels do not yield enough energy for photosynthesis. Shade cloth is often used to protect sensitive seedlings and plants from strong sun by partially blocking light and reducing the intensity.

Light quality is based on the wavelengths of visible light, which ranges from violet (the shortest wavelength) to red (the longest), with all the colors of the rainbow in between. Below violet there is the ultraviolet range, or UV light. Above red there is the far red and infrared. Photosynthetic pigments have evolved to interact with light at wavelengths of blue and red. The shorter blue wavelengths provide greater energy. Far-red light causes long, thin stems and also triggers the transfer from vegetative growth to flowering. Placement in the garden affects the quality of sunlight that reaches the plant, as sunlight coming in at an angle closer to the horizon contains less high-energy blue light than sunlight arriving by a shorter overhead path.

Flowering in angiosperms is triggered by night length. **Photoperiod** is a term that describes the relative numbers of hours of daylight and darkness. Night begins with far-red light at dusk and ends with far-red light at dawn and these wavelengths are involved in the plant's ability to keep track of the length of the night. Some plants have specific requirements as to how long the period of darkness must last in order to trigger flowering. It is called the critical night length and it appears to be measured by a pigment found in leaves. Those plants that have evolved to bloom when the days are long and the nights are shorter (as in the late spring and early summer) are called long day/short night plants. Many annual plants belong to this group. Some wait for shorter days with longer nights, like chrysanthemums, which can bloom in the late fall or even winter; these are the short day/long night plants. Some plants, such as roses and geraniums, are not controlled by the photoperiod and are considered day neutral. In this case, flowering is controlled by other factors.

Natural daylight ranges from 8 hours at winter solstice to 14 hours at summer solstice. Ancient calendars marked the solstices with physical structures. If you know when solstice is, you know when to plant vegetables to ensure harvest before winter sets in. Knowledge of photoperiod requirements is also required to design flower gardens that will be in constant bloom from the spring through fall. Photoperiod can be manipulated by using infrared light, which is a strategy used to induce flowering in commercial greenhouses. This will be described in Chapter 6.

Light intensity and light quality are used to separate plants into groups that require full sun, part sun, part shade or shade. Full-sun plants like a full day of high-quality light, part-sun plants require 5 to 6 hours of high-quality light, part-shade plants need to get filtered light all day, and shade plants require full protection from strong sun all day. The light requirements for growth are included in seed catalogs and on the seed packet, as well as on the tag that accompanies a plant for sale in a garden center. The bloom time is also provided and may be reported as a month or season or in terms of the photoperiod.

SOIL

Soils are often described by their predominant minerals, such as sand, silt, or clay. Water drains quickly from sandy soils; they also tend to be low in nutrients. Clay soils are higher in nutrients but do not drain well and can be quite sticky. Soils that have a balanced mix of sand, silt, and clay particles are called loams. When a loam soil is mixed with 3%–5% organic matter, it has the ideal texture for cultivation of a garden because it provides adequate drainage and nutrients. Soils with less than 1% organic matter are not very fertile. Soils that are in the best condition for growing plants are said to have good **tilth**. The mix of minerals in the soil is referred to as the texture and can be determined by sending a sample to a soil testing laboratory. Soil structure also affects tilth. If a soil has been compacted due to heavy equipment, it will be more difficult for plant roots to spread.

Natural soils are evolving, dynamic entities that consist of minerals plus live microbes and decomposed organic matter.

Organic matter is the result of decomposed plant, insect, and animal matter plus the microbes that decompose it. Organic matter has been decomposed beyond recognition of the original material. It is black and crumbly and has the ability to hold large amounts of water and nutrients. It is often called humus or compost. The process of creating compost is called composting and is described in Chapter 6.

If the soil has an abundance of clay, compost is added in order to improve the tilth. Adding sand to clay soil is not recommended, as this produces a material similar to cement, which as you can well imagine is not very conducive to growing plants. Likewise, if the soil is silty or sandy the addition of compost will also improve the tilth. However, many wildflowers and some culinary herbs prefer to grow in nutrient-poor, sandy soil so how you amend your soil depends upon the soil you have to start with as well as what you want to grow in it.

There are 17 nutrients that plants require in order to grow. They are supplied by the air, water, and soil. Nutrients are elements used by growing plant cells to synthesize more cells and to help fuel physiological processes. These elements are cycled through the environment in a process called biogeochemistry. Biogeochemical transformations of elements are mediated by microbes that may derive energy for growth and/or nutrients from the transformation reactions.

Some nutrients are considered macronutrients because they are required in relatively large concentrations. Hydrogen comes from water; potassium and phosphorous come from the soil; and carbon, oxygen, and nitrogen come from the air. Sulfur, magnesium, and calcium are required in lower concentrations and also come from the soil. Other soil-derived nutrients that are required in even lower concentrations are called micronutrients or trace elements and include chlorine, iron, manganese, boron, copper, zinc, molybdenum, and cobalt. If any one of these nutrients is not present in the required amount, growth of the plant will be inhibited. This is known as Liebeg's Law of the Minimum. Too much of a good thing is not good in this case, as micronutrients can become toxic to plants when applied in excessive amounts. Silica, a major component of sand, is also believed to be an important mineral for plant growth.

Hydrogen is the most common element and is also an important macronutrient. It is a component of water that is found in soil pores. When water molecules (H_2O) split, as they often do, they generate positively charged hydrogen ions (H^+) and negatively charged hydroxy radicals (OH^-). A pH meter measures the number of hydrogen ions in a saturated soil and returns the value as a negative log function that ranges from 0 to 14. If there are an equal number of hydrogen ions and hydroxy radicals, the pH is neutral and has a value of 7. A pH of less than 7 is acidic; the lower the number, the more acidic it is. If the pH is greater than 7 the soil is said to be alkaline; the higher the number, the greater the alkalinity.

Most cultivated plants prefer a soil with a pH between 6.5 and 6.8 although a few tenths of a unit either way is usually tolerable. The reason for this has to do with the effect of pH on the availability of nutrients. When the soil pH is in this range, all of the nutrients are soluble and the plant can access them through its roots. When the pH is more alkaline or more acidic, some of the nutrients will form insoluble compounds that the plant cannot access even though they are present in the soil.

Minerals such as calcium, magnesium, potassium, and sodium contribute to alkalinity and are called soluble salts. They may be leached out of a soil that has formed in hot, humid conditions with high annual rainfall (tropical, subtropical). The soil becomes very acidic and may have problems with aluminum toxicity because aluminum changes to a soluble form at low pH and the plants can take it up through the roots.

Soluble salts tend to accumulate in arid and semiarid regions that are heavily irrigated—especially in poorly drained clay soils

Figure 4.2 The excessive use of fertilizers and irrigation in arid regions can cause overly alkaline soil. The alkalized soil forms a white crust of accumulated salts on the surface of the fields, which is toxic to most plants and detrimental to the land.

(Figure 4.2). Water evaporates quickly in these environments and the salts become concentrated in the upper layers of the soil. These soils are not good for growing a garden and may become home to microbial communities and plants that are adapted to the high salt concentration. Soils that have accumulated very high concentrations of some salts (such as sodium) are very difficult to bring into good tilth. Some plant breeders are working on the creation of hybrid crops that can withstand high salt concentrations.

Soil pH can be increased by adding lime, which is crushed limestone mined from quarries and contains calcium carbonate. Sometimes it is mixed with magnesium and called gypsum. The addition of wood ashes, which are high in potassium, also raises the pH of the soil. This needs to be done carefully, several months prior to planting to allow the chemical reactions to take place. Too much calcium or potassium can elevate the pH beyond what is tolerable to garden plants, and it may take years for the pH to lower again to a suitable range.

Sulfur lowers the pH of the soil. Organic amendments such as pine needles and peat moss also lower the pH. The amount to use depends upon the pH of your soil, the size of the area you need to cover, and what you plan to grow. Some plants such as blueberries and azaleas prefer a soil pH of 6.0, more acidic than for most garden plants. Soil test results can indicate the appropriate rate of application of materials to alter the pH of your soil for the particular plants you intend to grow. Soil test results can also indicate whether you need to add nutrients and in what amounts.

If your compost and mineral soil do not supply enough nutrients, you may need to supplement with fertilizer. There are many fertilizers on the market. Organic and chemical fertilizers are formulated to supply a mix of the three nutrients required in abundance, which are nitrogen (N), phosphorous (P) and potassium (K). The amount of fertilizer is shown on the label as a ratio of N-P-K. Some fertilizers are formulated to supply the micronutrients as trace minerals. Chemical nitrogen fertilizers are generated by the conversion of nitrogen gas in the air to a soluble powdered form. This process requires energy because the gaseous nitrogen bonds are difficult to split. Rock phosphate is a substance mined from the ground; large supplies are found in Florida. Rock phosphate supplies high phosphorous and also adds calcium. Greensand is from ancient seabed deposits and is a source of potassium and many trace minerals. Seaweed is also high in potassium.

Organic fertilizers such as blood meal and fish meal also supply high nitrogen. They come from slaughterhouses and processing plants. If you prefer not to use animal products, legumes such as soybean meal and alfalfa meal can be used as a nitrogen fertilizer. Many growers plant alfalfa to increase the nitrogen in the soil. Home gardeners often plant peas or beans, which are also legumes.

Plants have different requirements for nutrients at different stages of growth. Nitrogen promotes vegetative growth and too much may result in poor flower and fruit formation. Phosphorous stimulates root growth and flower production and is useful to add to a new transplant and when plants begin to flower. Potassium is required in the transport of nutrients and also is involved in **turgor pressure** and **transpiration.**

WATER

The water found in the pores of the soil is called the soil solution and carries dissolved nutrients as well as microbial life. Water is necessary to transfer soluble nutrients to all parts of the plant and must be present in sufficient quantities for the elongation of plant cells that contribute to growth. In waterlogged soils, water molecules displace the soil air that contains oxygen. This causes lower respiration rates in the roots and can actually decrease the ability of the plant to take up water from the soil, which causes the plant to wilt.

Rainwater is slightly acidic because of the carbon dioxide naturally present in the atmosphere and may become even more acidic as a result of pollution. Rain is also a transport vehicle for microbes that are swept into the atmosphere. If there is insufficient rainfall for healthy plants, a supplemental source is required. Commercial growers may have access to surface water, such as ponds and rivers with irrigation ditches used to divert water to the crops. They may also use a sprinkler system. Alternatively, wells are often used to supply irrigation water and are preferred because the water is less likely to transmit disease.

Water quality should be tested prior to planting. If the water supply is from surface water or a well, this can be done by sending a water sample to a laboratory. You want to check for pH, mineral content, and soluble salts, as well as toxic chemicals that could injure your plants. If you are using municipal tap water to water plants, you should ask the county or municipality for a water quality report, which they should provide to you at no charge. High levels of chlorine or fluoride in tap water may injure your plants. If your water is not good, you can invest in equipment to purify it.

The method used to irrigate water may depend upon climate, the size of the garden, and proximity to the water source. One method is to irrigate from overhead and the other is to provide water directly to the root zone. Fertilizer is sometimes applied dissolved in the irrigation water; this is referred to as fertigation. There are advantages and drawbacks to both methods.

Overhead water washes off leaves and may help deter foliage pests, but water can be lost to evaporation and may not reach the roots, especially in hot, dry weather. Overhead rinses with organic amendments such as compost tea or kelp extracts have been reported to increase plant vigor. Pivot irrigation is an overhead sprinkler system that projects water out from a central source in a circular motion moving like the hands on a clock, which results in a circular patch of irrigated land that looks like big green circles when viewed from overhead (Figure 4.3).

When plants are exposed to a frost, an early morning rinse with water to wash frost off the leaves will prevent damage as long as the leaves have not yet been exposed to sunlight. Plants can be protected from frost by covering them with cloth or plastic or by moving potted plants to a sheltered area. Your local weather report will give you notice if a frost is expected overnight.

Water applied directly to the root zone by drip irrigation concentrates the water by the roots where the plant can access it. Drip irrigation delivers water through a soaker hose, which is perforated. This method is more easily applied in the small garden

Figure 4.3 Center pivot irrigation creates circular farms such as the ones seen above. Center pivot irrigation is a type of crop irrigation in which equipment rotates around a fixed point. Computer-controlled center pivot irrigation systems allow farmers to operate from a remote location.

than in large commercial fields, which may have problems with clogging. The hose is laid on the ground close to the stems of your plants and can be covered with mulch to reduce evaporation.

Water that is applied too late in the day, close to dusk, or after nightfall may create problems because of conditions that favor the growth of fungi. Many types of fungi thrive in cool, moist conditions and reproduce with spores. The spores are

Plant Water Requirements

How much water does a plant need? That depends upon the plant, the climate, and the rate of transpiration. Transpiration is the passage of water as a vapor from the leaf to the atmosphere. Water molecules move from areas of higher concentration to areas of lower concentration. High temperatures, low humidity, and wind can increase the rate of transpiration because they remove water from the air. If there is less water in the air than in the plant leaf, water will move from the plant into the air.

Plants that do not receive adequate water intake through the roots during times of increased transpiration may wilt, and if the conditions persist, they will die. The amount of water required varies among species that have evolved in climates with different amounts of rainfall. Plants that are native to arid and semiarid regions have modified leaves and stems that conserve water and reduce transpiration. These plants are sometimes referred to as drought tolerant or xeric.

Plants that are native to tropical regions with warm, moist air tend to have broad leaves that shed water and may transpire at a higher rate than xeric plants when exposed to hot, dry weather. High transpiration combined with evaporation dries out the soil. Plant water requirements are often listed as low, moderate, or high, with xeric plants at the low end and tropical plants at the high end. Plants with shallow lateral roots are usually not drought tolerant and require more frequent water than plants with deep taproots, which will do well even if the soil dries out between watering.

transported in water. It is important to avoid working in a wet garden, as this can spread microbial diseases that are in water droplets. The spores can become attached to your shoes, gloves, or tools and cause you to infect other plants. It is not a good idea to transfer garden tools from one place to another unless they are sterilized between uses, as residue left on tools can spread microbial diseases. Wet soil can also be easily compacted by footsteps or heavy machinery, which makes it harder for plants to grow.

CLIMATE

The climate of a particular region is based on annual average high and low temperatures, annual rainfall, and the number of frost-free days. Wind and altitude are modifiers. Linnaeus said that altitude is more in accordance with the habitation of plants than latitude or longitude. This is backed up by research that found that plants growing in alpine regions are similar in different parts of the world, whereas plants growing at the same longitude or latitude are often different.

The USDA has generated climate maps that divide the country into zones based on climate. The United States National Arboretum Web site listed in the Further Reading section has an interactive USDA Plant Hardiness Zone Map that you can access to determine the zone for your region. It also provides information on how to choose perennial plants that will survive the winter in your area.

SUMMARY

This chapter described how plant physiological processes such as photosynthesis, respiration, and transpiration are tied to a plant's cultural requirements. Sunshine, soil, and water provide the plant with nutrients and energy for growth. Plants differ in terms of the quality and quantity of sun, water, and nutrients they require, and also in their preferred soil texture. The horticulturist's job is to provide plants with the highest quality light, water, and soil possible in accordance with their individual needs. Growers must be aware of the cultural requirements of each of the plants in the garden. The next chapter presents the interactions between plants and other organisms and how they may be beneficial or detrimental to the garden.

5 Ecology and Pest Management

Ecology and Pest Management

Let's suppose that you have done all your homework and are familiar with the cultural requirements of your favorite plants. You have started a garden and your plants are growing great. Then one morning, after six weeks of hard work, you go to water your vegetables and all the leaves are gone. What if it was a commercial crop and now you have nothing to sell? The protection of plants from hungry pests is an age-old problem. Integrated pest management (IPM) is a decision-making process that is used to manage organisms that are harmful to the garden and is based on a fundamental knowledge of ecology. It applies an integrated approach of chemical, biological, mechanical, and cultural controls.

Plants interact with insects, animals, microbes, and other plants. Some insects, animals, and microbes are beneficial to the garden and others are destructive. Nonbiological factors such as climate and soil conditions affect the ecological balance of the garden. For example, an unusually cold, wet summer can promote fungal infections in plants. Alternatively, dry and dusty conditions may contribute to outbreaks of destructive plant-eating mites. This chapter introduces some of the beneficial and harmful aspects of the interactions that may occur between plants and other organisms in either the rhizosphere (below ground) or the phyllosphere (above ground).

THE RHIZOSPHERE

The rhizosphere is the area in the soil around the plant roots. It consists of soil, insects, microbes, and roots. Some soil fauna, such as spiders and their relatives, the mites, are not true insects and are called arachnids. They have eight legs. Spiders do not eat plants; they eat insects that hurt the garden. Other creatures, such as slugs and snails, are also found in the soil and feed on plants. Microbes are organisms that are too small to be viewed without a microscope and include bacteria, viruses, fungi, protists, algae, and nematodes.

Figure 5.1 Earthworms are an important component to composting. In vermicomposting, or worm composting, red earthworms are used to consume and digest organic matter in order to produce castings, an odor-free soil additive.

Some soil microbes are opportunistic pathogens. They do not affect healthy plants, but if a plant is weakened by environmental conditions, the microbe will enter the plant and cause infection. Beneficial soil microbes make nutrients available to plants and in exchange get carbohydrates from the plants. Beneficial rhizosphere microbes are also responsible for the generation of compost from animal and plant matter. Earthworms are also helpful in the composting process and in the recycling of nutrients (Figure 5.1). Worms should not be introduced into ecosystems where they are not naturally found, however, because they can cause extensive damage to the organic layer in forests and reduce the habitat for native creatures.

Composting of green plants directly in the soil is known as green manuring. Green manures are usually supplied from young weeds that have been mechanically removed with a hoe and turned back into the soil to decompose. Some growers plant a cold-tolerant cereal or legume crop that grows over the winter and then turn it into the soil in the spring. The soil microbes break down the plant and recycle the nutrients into the soil.

The nutrient that is most often deficient in the soil is nitrogen. Soil microbes that belong to the genus *Rhizobium* form nodules on the roots of legumes and convert nitrogen from the atmosphere into a form that becomes soluble in the soil and available for plant uptake. Free-living nitrogen-fixing bacteria such as *Azospirillum* and *Cyanobacteria* are also found naturally in the soil.

Mycorrhizal fungi form long hyphal filaments that stretch into the soil in search of nutrients; they also form associations with plant roots. The fungi bring nutrients such as phosphorous to the plant in exchange for carbohydrates and may also protect the plant from fungal pathogens. Additionally, the hypha helps to bind the soil particles together and give the soil good tilth. Many plants form symbiotic associations with mycorrhizal fungi. Plants that are normally found in association with mycorrhizal fungi will not thrive if they do not form the association. It may take years to establish the associations, which are very important in forested and natural ecosystems. Wildflowers often die if you try to dig them up in the wild and plant them in your garden, because their symbiotic mychorrhizal fungi do not survive the trip.

Some soil bacteria, such as *Streptomyces*, produce antibiotics that kill other microbes. *Streptomyces* also produce a substance called geosmin that is responsible for the earthy smell of garden soil and ripened compost. Bacteria from the genera *Bacillus* and *Pseudomonas* are used to kill fungal pathogens. They are added to seeds or sterilized potting media and are labeled and treated as fungicides. These organisms are naturally present in fertile soil and in properly aged compost, so there should be no need to purchase them if you add high-quality compost to your garden.

Fungal and viral diseases can be spread by water droplets that bounce off the soil and land on leaves. The use of plastic mulch for plants that are susceptible to viral diseases has given good results. The mulch creates a barrier between the soil and the leaves. Many other types of mulch, such as cedar or pine bark (which smells like the trees), are available. They are yellow or reddish in color. Cocoa mulch smells like chocolate and has a dark brown color. Gravel is also sometimes used, especially with drought-tolerant plants. Straw and hay are very popular and can be easily picked up and moved when needed, although you have to be careful that the hay does not contain weed seeds.

Mulch should not be placed too close to the stem, as overly moist conditions may lead to fungal infections. Mulch is used to lessen temperature fluctuations and to conserve water in the soil and prevent erosion. Temperature affects plants at all stages of growth. The temperature of the surface of the soil, where plant growth occurs, may fluctuate widely over daily and annual (season-to-season) intervals.

Crop rotations also help because disease organisms can survive the winter in the soil. Many disease-causing microbes and insects are specific about which plants they will infect. If no host plants are available for a few years, the pathogen population will die back from lack of a host. Crops that grow in the same place year after year can cause an increase in the insect pest population in the soil. This is why growers who practice monocropping often use large quantities of insecticides. For example, conventional commercial strawberry growers used to routinely fumigate the soil with methyl bromide to kill disease microbes as well as weeds.

Figure 5.2 A weed called giant foxtail grows between rows of corn on the right-hand side of this photograph. The corn on the left has been treated with an herbicide that prevents foxtail growth. Weeds compete with crops for nutrients and water, and they spread diseases.

This substance has been recently banned by the EPA, however, because it is toxic to humans and depletes ozone. It also kills the beneficial organisms in the soil.

Weeds are plants that grow in a place where you do not want them to be, such as in a vegetable garden or in the middle of a lawn. Many weeds are escaped garden plants from European settlers that are no longer in fashion or foreign grasses that hitched a ride in grain shipments. Weeds compete with garden plants for nutrients and water and may cause overcrowding and lead to conditions that spread disease (Figure 5.2).

Weeds can be pulled by hand or scraped off the surface with a hoe. Hoes have a sharp edge that is used to remove the weed just below the surface of the soil. Any weeded plants that are not edible can either be turned back into the soil as green manure or put into a compost heap. Plants release compounds from their roots into the soil. Some of these are weak acids that help to release nutrients from the soil. Plants also can release allelochemicals that affect other plants. Some weeds, such as tamarisk and knapweed, produce chemicals that prevent the growth of other plants.

Herbicides are chemicals used to kill weeds and are widely applied by both commercial growers and home gardeners, especially on lawns. Some target the broad leaf dicot plants but allow the monocot grasses to continue to grow, whereas others may target the monocot grasses. Misuse of commonly used herbicides can result in contamination of water supplies and may be toxic to humans. They are not used in organic horticulture, as mechanical methods of weed removal are effective and the weeds are a source of compost material. Weeds can be prevented by the use of smother crops, which are planted in between rows or in other places where weeds might grow.

THE PHYLLOSPHERE

Phyllosphere is a term used to refer to the environment in the areas of the aboveground portions of a plant, especially the leaves. It attracts many insects. The study of insects is called entomology and a horticulturist must learn to recognize the beneficial and harmful insects in a garden. Insect pollinators are beneficial. Insects that eat plant parts are destructive. Common destructive insects are mealy bugs, aphids, white flies, thrips, caterpillars, and grasshoppers. Plant viruses are often spread from plant to plant by aphids and thrips, as well as mealybugs and some leafhoppers, so you need to watch for signs of viral infections in plants that have been infested with these insects.

Daily walks through the garden, greenhouse, or commercial field will alert you to potential insect infestations before they get out of hand. This is one of the responsibilities of the greenhouse or farm manager. If plants become heavily infested, physical

Composting: How to Make Black Gold

Compost, the black crumbly material that remains after decomposition of plant residues and animal manures, is worth its weight in gold to the organic or sustainable grower, but it must be of good quality. Compost heaps can be made directly on the ground or in containers. A source of microbial inoculation, such as soil or commercially available compost starter, is also required. A proper mix of carbon and nitrogen in the starting materials is very important. Straw and dried leaves are high in carbon and are often combined in layers with grass clippings or kitchen scraps, which are high in nitrogen. Straw also helps to keep air in the pile, which encourages aerobic decomposition and prevents the formation of noxious gases. Growers may also add fresh animal manure or fish scraps to the compost pile as a source of nitrogen. Fresh manure is not appropriate for direct application to the garden, as it is too strong and may burn plant roots or spread disease-causing microbes such as *E. coli.* Manure sources should be investigated, as some farmers give their animals high quantities of antibiotics that can inhibit microbial decomposition.

The composting process takes about six months but is sensitive to cold temperatures. A correctly built compost pile heats up to more than 60°C. This high heat kills pathogens and weed seeds while special microbes adapted to the high temperature continue the decomposition process. The pile should be turned regularly to rotate freshly added materials into the center of the pile and keep it aerated. After the temperature stabilizes and cools, the compost should ripen prior to addition to the garden. Municipal compost piles may include sewage sludge, the residue from sewage treatment facilities, which contains concentrated toxic heavy metals, such as cadmium, mercury, and lead. There are strict EPA regulations with regard to how much composted sewage sludge can be applied to the soil. Compost made with sludge should be avoided by home gardeners.

Figure 5.3 Lady beetles, also known as ladybugs, feed on aphids, which are a common garden pest.

methods may be used to remove the insect pest. These methods can include the application of water or shaking the plant over a container to catch the insects as they fall. If it is a localized infestation of annual plants, the affected plants are removed from the garden. If the plants are perennial, other options to rid the plants of the pest may be tried before removal. Texts on organic gardening can be consulted for advice on a particular problem.

Predatory insects and spiders that feed on destructive insects are beneficial to the garden (Figure 5.3). Lady beetles (commonly called ladybugs), parasitic wasps, spiders, lacewings, syrphide flies, damsel bugs, assassin bugs, and minute pirate bugs are all beneficials. Beneficial insects can be encouraged to live and eat in the garden if there is a high diversity of plants and the use of insecticides is avoided—many insecticides do not discriminate between the harmful and beneficial insects.

Some species of beneficial insects may be purchased for intentional release into a field or greenhouse. This is known as biological control and is a relatively new method. Microbes can also be purchased for use in biological control. *Bacillus thuringiensis* (Bt) is a commonly used microbial biological control. Experiments are underway to determine how effective the intentional release of insects and microbes are for commercial applications. Other creatures such as birds, toads, reptiles, bats, snakes, and rodents also eat harmful insects.

Trap crops are plants that are not intended for harvest but supply habitat for insects and are planted along the perimeter of a garden. In the foothills of northern Colorado, the wild sunflower plants and native yucca are good examples of trap crops. Trap crops can provide a breeding ground for beneficial insects that feed on pests. This ensures a high population of beneficials available to protect your crop during the growing season.

Companion crops sometimes work because some plants produce chemicals that are a deterrent to the insect pest of the crop you plant next to it. The scent of the companion plant may overwhelm the scent of the crop that the insect is attracted to such that the insect is unable to find its food source. Other scents may be unpleasant enough that the insect stays away from the area. For example, French marigolds and basil emit a scent that deters many insect pests and are often planted among vegetable plants in the garden as companions.

Staggered planting is the strategy of planting a crop earlier or later in the season than usual to confound the insect pest that is expecting to find it at a particular time. This works for crops that are day neutral and do not rely on the day length to initiate flowering. Tomatoes are one example.

Commercial growers may find that insecticides are necessary to save a crop in distress, but it is important to identify the underlying cause of the infestation and try to correct it. Sometimes the methods used, such as monocropping and amendments that reduce the tilth of the soil, are the crux of the problem. Insecticides may require that you obtain a pesticide license before you can apply them. Since they are toxic, they require a safe place for storage and may require special disposal methods. They may also require special equipment to apply. Many insecticides persist in the soil or contaminate water supplies. Also, insecticides can be expensive.

ANIMAL PESTS

Animals such as rabbits, deer, and birds may eat flowers, leaves, and fruits, and gophers eat bulbs—all of which can leave you angry and frustrated. Animals are particularly fond of plants that are well fertilized and watered frequently, because they are more tasty and nutritious than the wild plants. There are several ways that gardeners have handled this problem.

The first way is to exclude the animals from your garden. This is most effectively done with garden walls or fences. Deer are capable of jumping quite high, so the structure has to be about 8 feet (2.4 meters) tall. Netting with a mesh small enough to keep out birds can be placed over the tops of plants when fruits begin to ripen. It is more difficult to exclude gophers with this method, although you could plant your bulbs in containers that are buried in the ground to prevent the gophers from reaching them.

A second way to exclude animal pests is to trick them into thinking that a predator is near. Fox, coyote, and big-cat urine obtained from zoos has been reported to deter rabbits and deer, who fear the presence of these predators. Scarecrows, shiny reflective objects, ribbons, statues that look like owls or hawks, and bits of hose that look like snakes have also been used to scare birds. A well-behaved dog that intimidates animal grazers but that does not trample your garden may also be effective.

A third method is to spray some kind of concoction on the plants that gives them a disagreeable taste. There are many formulas on the market and homemade recipes that can be tried, but they need to be reapplied after it rains. A fourth option uses mechanical means that are activated by motion detectors to chase away animals. These include electric fences, alarms, and sprinklers.

Lastly, there are plants that deer and rabbits prefer to avoid. Deer in some regions may eat plants that they will not touch in other areas. This may be reflective of the soil and its effect on the plant, or it may be due to lack of more desirable food plants. During a particularly severe winter, deer may resort to eating plants they normally would not go near.

MAINTENANCE

The real science in horticulture comes from observations and record keeping. Taking notes on daily or weekly walks through the garden during the growing season is highly recommended. These notes can include information on any observed insect damage, nutrient deficiencies, microbial diseases, or weeds. It is also necessary to keep a record of any treatments that you apply, and the results. These notes will help you make decisions about changes that you may need to make for the following year.

It is most important to remember that you remove nutrients from the soil by harvesting plants and that you must return nutrients to the soil. Plants that do not receive sufficient nutrients are more prone to attack by insects and microbial diseases. On the other hand, soils that are overfertilized have a reduction in the beneficial microbes that recycle nutrients and help prevent disease. Regular maintenance and **best management practices** that limit the amount of chemical fertilizers help to keep plants healthy.

Organic gardeners build up the soil with regular incorporation of compost and keep the pH in a range between 6.5 and 6.8

to ensure plant-available nutrients. Compost can be sprinkled onto the garden and does not have to be dug in. You can also sprinkle compost on your lawn. When you mow your lawn, you should allow the clippings to stay there. This returns nutrients and lessens the need for the addition of nitrogen fertilizer.

Exposed soil often forms a hard, crusty surface as water evaporates. The next time you water or the next time it rains, the water will run off the hard surface instead of penetrating into the soil. This is desirable in the desert, where desert crusts develop bacterial communities that prevent erosion and add nutrients to the soil. In the garden, the crust needs to be broken up and turned into the soil. A garden tool called a cultivator has metal prongs that are used to break up the hard surface of the soil. Adding mulch to the top of your exposed soil can prevent this crust from forming.

Many herbaceous flowering plants bloom longer if they are deadheaded. When the bloom begins to wither, it is removed from the plant and added it to the compost heap. Decaying blooms and dead leaves are susceptible to gray rot, a fungal disease with a fuzzy gray appearance caused by *Botrytis cinerea* (Figure 5.4).

Purchased plants have to be inspected for pests such as mealy bugs, mites, white flies, or aphids because they can be transferred to your garden. Plants that are spindly, wilted, or have damaged leaves may carry microbial diseases and should not be bought.

Plants should not be crowded closely together, as this promotes the spread of fungal diseases through poor air circulation. The garden should be thinned as it is growing to allow plants room to spread. The recommended distances between plants are provided on seed packets or tags with transplants. Thinning involves removing weaker crop plants or weeds to allow the larger, healthy crop plants room to grow. Perennial plants must be divided every few years; otherwise they will get too crowded

Figure 5.4 *Botrytis cinerea* grows on a young petunia plant. Plant diseases caused by Botrytis fungi commonly infect vegetables, ornamentals, fruits, and some field crops. It is one of the most frequent causes of infection in greenhouse plants. Spread of the disease can be controlled by the removal of the dead or dying leaves and flowers.

and decline in health. They are dug up either in the spring or fall, depending on the cultivar, then are separated and replanted.

Climbing plants need to be provided with a structure to climb. Fruiting plants are more prone to disease if they are lying in the soil. Crops such as peas, beans, squash, and cucumbers can be trained to climb lengths of nylon string that have been attached to a wooden frame, or on a trellis. Crops such as raspberries and grapes need to have support structures as well. Tomatoes usually require staking, as do many tall flowering plants. The weight of the fruit or flower may cause the stems to droop. Therefore, they are attached loosely to a stake.

Woody ornamental plants are pruned once a year or less often to remove dead branches, and sometimes live branches, to change the shape. Pruning is accomplished with a tool called pruning shears, which comes in various sizes to accommodate plants with branches of different diameters. Small saws are used on tree limbs. Trees and shrubs can be damaged if they are not pruned correctly. Fact sheets on the maintenance of woody plants are readily available through the horticultural extension service.

SUMMARY

This chapter presented the interactions that plants have with other plants, microbes, insects, other soil fauna, and animals. Maintenance of good tilth and a balanced garden ecology can go a long way to prevent many pest problems. If you are realistic about what to expect from your garden and somewhat tolerant of the creatures that share your garden space, you will derive more pleasure and less frustration from your efforts. Some of the challenges faced by commercial growers, as well as harvest and post-harvest methods and techniques for greenhouse production, are discussed in the next chapter.

6 Commercial Horticulture

We abuse land because we regard it as a commodity belonging to us. When we see land as a community to which we belong, we may begin to use it with love and respect.

–Aldo Leopold (1887–1948)
American ecologist

Commercial Horticulture

Next time you eat a french fry, think about where the potato came from. Most of us are completely dependent on commercial horticulture to supply us with seeds, plants, produce, flowers, herbs, and all the products that are derived from them. We expect high-quality products at an affordable price. So what do you think are the biggest challenges to commercial horticulture and what can be done about them? Two of the greatest concerns are the access to good quality natural resources: water and soil. Other problems are the potential for catastrophic crop loss due to disease or bioterrorism, and international competition that drives down prices and makes it increasingly difficult for commercial farms to make a profit.

Well water is preferred for irrigation because it is usually of a higher quality than surface water from ponds, lakes, or rivers, which can contain pathogens. Excessive use of groundwater through heavy irrigation causes **geologic** problems, such as those seen in California, Texas, Arizona, and some of the states surrounding the Gulf of Mexico. One of the best examples is seen in the experience of Mexico City. The water is withdrawn by wells from **aquifers** at a rate that is faster than the recharge of the aquifers by **precipitation** and **percolation;** if the **soil pores** that were once filled with water collapse, the aquifer cannot be recharged, the wells run dry, and the land sinks.

The rate of water withdrawal from the Colorado River and the current drought, combined with population growth in the sunny, warm regions of the Southwest, further endangers freshwater supplies and wreaks havoc on the environment. Commercial horticulture tends to follow the sun because warmer climates mean longer growing seasons, but there simply is not enough water to go around and the poor Colorado River is drained dry before it ever reaches the ocean. Additionally, heavy irrigation of soil in semiarid and arid regions creates problems with salination and poor soil fertility similar to those that caused the downfall of ancient Mesopotamian, Egyptian, Greek, and Roman agricultural productivity.

As urban sprawl encroaches on agricultural land, there are conflicts. The well-drained loamy soils that are perfect for growing crops are also ideal for building houses, and it is very tempting for a farmer who is barely getting by to sell the land to the highest bidder. When residential neighborhoods come into contact with farmland, there are concerns with dangers associated with pesticide drift and drinking water contamination. Across the United States, prime farmland is being turned into housing developments. Increased pressure for biofuels (such as ethanol, which is made from corn) may translate into even more land taken away from food production, with a corresponding increase in the amount of chemical fertilizers and herbicides applied.

The frozen-food industry often contracts with farmers to grow specific cultivars because the plants yield fruits or vegetables of a consistent size and quality that can be readily processed by their manufacturing equipment. One example is the Russet potato, the cultivar bred by Luther Burbank, which is the perfect size and has the best consistency for making french fries (Figure 6.1). The problem is that this potato cultivar is also prone to disease. Heavy applications of pesticides are required to produce a crop acceptable to factory owners. This is not in the best interests of the farmer, because land abused with heavy applications of chemical fertilizers and pesticides becomes less fertile over time and can endanger the health of the farmer. Other types of potatoes are disease resistant and do not require the pesticide use, but the factory wants the Russets so the farmer either produces them or loses the contract. Factory farms are one reason that farmers practice monocropping.

A problem with monocropping is the reduction in the genetic diversity of our food crops. High diversity means that a crop

Figure 6.1 Technicians inspect Russet potatoes, the potato of choice for french fry processors.

has many different varieties. Some of these may have traits for resistance to a particular disease. The lower the diversity of our food crops, the more susceptible they are to outbreaks of natural diseases or bioterrorism. Low crop diversity has led to catastrophic failure as a result of disease, because all the plants are susceptible to the same pathogens. The corn blight of 1970 wiped out most of the nation's corn crop because growers all planted the same variety, which could not resist this microbial infection. **Seed gene banks** store genetic diversity for breeding new hybrids of important food crops, but unless diverse crops are planted in the field, a single disease can wipe out entire harvests.

All of this sounds quite dreadful, but many commercial growers are implementing sustainable methods to overcome these problems and legislatures across the country are taking steps to conserve farmland and good freshwater. There is a long way to go. Consumer demand for organically grown produce helps to put pressure on the food processing industry, which in turn may help farmers who want to plant more diverse crops and reduce pesticide use.

GREENHOUSE CROPS

One way to decrease the need for soil and water resources is with greenhouse production (Figure 6.2), although not all crops may be suitable for this. Greenhouse crops such as tomatoes, cucumbers, lettuce, peppers, herbs, and strawberries are grown with hydroponics. Technically, the term *hydroponic* describes plants grown in water that has been amended with soluble nutrients, but now it is also often used to describe plants grown in some type of sterilized material to give the roots a place to anchor. These materials can be gravel, sand, or rock wool, which is spun fibers from melted rocks that have been compressed into cubes or slabs. The benefits of hydroponic versus field-grown crops are lower water use, less disease, fewer fertilizers required, less labor, reduced need for pesticides, less damage to the environment, and

Figure 6.2 Traditional greenhouse production of plants involves over-head irrigation as opposed to the method described in the text for hydro-ponics. Greenhouses allow for a controlled environment unsusceptible to harsh weather conditions, but plants are still prone to insect infestations and microbial diseases and must be carefully monitored.

higher yield. Water is kept in a closed system and recycled. The nutrient levels and pH of the water are closely monitored and adjusted as needed. The water can be reused for many months.

Another similar method is the ebb and flow system used with potted plants. The pots are filled with a sterilized media composed of various combinations of peat moss, pine bark, **vermiculite,** or sand. Beneficial microbes that help prevent pathogens from causing disease are often inoculated into the potting media. Organic growers may use well-ripened compost that has been sieved through a small mesh screen. The pots are kept in large, waterproof plastic trays, which are periodically flooded with water. The plants absorb the water from the bottom of the pot by capillary action in the roots and the excess water is drained into a reservoir container and recycled for many months.

Hydroponic and ebb and flow methods can be modified to meet many of the requirements for organic or sustainable certification and they are less degrading to the environment than conventional agriculture in the field. However, not all greenhouses are pesticide free. Insect infestations in the greenhouse may be more difficult to deal with than outdoors in the field because predatory insects and other creatures that normally consume these pest insects cannot get in to feed.

Plants infected with viruses or other microbial infections are susceptible to insect infestations, and fungal infections are common. Therefore, many commercial greenhouses regularly spray insecticides. Many of these chemicals persist on greenhouse benches, on plants, and on the floor. Commercial greenhouses have a dedicated quarantine area that is used to hold new plants for a few weeks prior to their introduction into the greenhouse. This is to allow time to observe and remove any pests that may have hitched a ride, before they get into the greenhouse.

Sticky cards colored blue or yellow are often used to monitor and trap harmful insects, especially thrips and whiteflies, in the greenhouse. The insects are attracted to the colorful cards and get stuck to the surface. Additionally, **pheromone** traps may be helpful. Insects release pheromones to lure members of the opposite sex; these can be used to entice pests into the traps.

Insufficient sunlight may cause problems with plant growth and development. Sunlight in greenhouse structures made of glass is at 89% of unobstructed light. Polyethylene double-pane plastic transmits 84%. Greenhouses must be kept clean to transmit this amount of light. Plastic also transmits less light when it is scratched. Rain cleans the outside of a greenhouse, but the inside must be regularly maintained and kept free of plant debris and standing water. Disease is spread through standing water on the floors and from fallen leaves and withered flowers that may harbor Botrytis mold spores.

Plants need protection from high-intensity light during the summer, so shade cloth or whitewash is used on the windows to block some of the light. The greenhouse must also have an adequate ventilation system since good air circulation is required to prevent diseases. Carbon dioxide, which is required for photosynthesis, may become depleted if the greenhouse is closed during inclement weather. Injection of carbon dioxide into the closed greenhouse can increase photosynthesis and speed up the time to harvest as long as there is sufficient light. The amount of carbon dioxide required to increase plant growth is not high enough to cause any problems to humans who breathe the air.

The temperature in the greenhouse is crucial and must be within the range required for the crops. Heating costs are higher in cooler climates. Locations near the equator have longer growing seasons and more hours of sunlight, and thus have no need to heat the greenhouses during the winter. As a result, they can offer greenhouse crops at a lower cost. International competition has been particularly tough on the American cut-flower industry because these crops can be efficiently transported over long distances with minimal damage.

FLORICULTURE

Long stem roses, the national flower of America, and carnations are two examples of cut-flower crops grown in the greenhouse. Roses are grown in beds on the floor of greenhouses and the plants produce cuttings for about 5 years. The roses receive a full day of natural sunlight, and specialized lightbulbs extend the total amount of light up to 18 hours per day. This way, the plants can be cut four times a year and harvests are timed for Christmas, Valentine's Day, Easter, and Mother's Day.

Flowering potted plants include poinsettias, marketed around the winter holidays, and geraniums that are very popular from Mother's Day through Memorial Day. Poinsettias may have their photoperiod manipulated by bursts of infrared light in order to time the bloom for the holidays. Green plants—which are sometimes called foliage plants or houseplants and include philodendrons, ficus, and ferns—are also grown for sale in pots or hanging baskets.

Bedding plants are raised for sale to consumers who plant them in their gardens or window boxes and include about 50 different types of flowers and vegetables (Figure 6.3). These crops are started in plastic trays called plugs, which are mechanically watered and fertilized. The seedlings are transferred into the flats, small containers, or small pots that are found at the garden center.

HARVEST AND POSTHARVEST

Crops are grown with one ultimate purpose in mind: the harvest. Harvest can begin shortly after planting if you consider that when you thin root crops such as carrots, you can eat the small baby carrots. Leafy greens such as lettuce or spinach can be harvested leaf by leaf as needed for salads. Chives and other herbs are also harvested as needed throughout the growing season.

Year-round harvest can be achieved with careful planning. Crops are planted continually, every three weeks or so, to prevent all the plants from maturing at the same time. Cold-season crops

Figure 6.3 Bedding plants are often grown in greenhouses, such as at the Plantorium in LaPorte, Colorado, pictured above.

that are given some protection with a cold frame can be left in the ground well into the winter in cooler climates and harvested when needed.

Fruits are harvested as they ripen. Commercially grown fruits may be stored in controlled environments with a higher ratio of carbon dioxide than found in the air to inhibit ripening. These must be specialized rooms that are entered wearing protective equipment because the air is not healthy to breathe. Ethylene is a gas used to induce ripening in apples, tomatoes, and bananas. It is also used to harvest commercially grown pineapples, black-berries, blueberries, and cherries. Rotten apples produce high amounts of ethylene and can cause other fruits that are stored with them to overripen. Therefore, it is best to store apples separately from other fruits.

Crops may be harvested by hand (for example, tomatoes, which are prone to damage) or by specialized machines (such as bean pickers) that have been designed specifically for that purpose. Crops fresh from the field may still be warmed from the sun and have what is called field heat. The heat present in the plant causes rapid decay after harvest and can be reduced by harvesting early in the day and immediately storing the produce in a cooler.

Postharvest handling of the fruit or vegetable differs for each crop. Some may need to be dried prior to storage. Crops that have soil on them should be washed thoroughly prior to drying. Perishable crops, like leafy greens, last longer if they are stored in a refrigerator with the stems in a container of water and a plastic bag placed over the top. Harvested produce that is not sold fresh or dried may be frozen, canned, fermented, or pickled. Frozen foods have become more popular in recent years than canned goods, although canning is still the preferred method for preserving tomatoes.

SUMMARY

This chapter covered the problems associated with soil and water used for commercial horticulture and some of the ways they may be overcome. Greenhouse produce and floriculture crops, and harvest and postharvest handling of crops, were also introduced. The following chapter presents some guidelines for residential garden design.

*For thee the wonder-working earth
puts forth sweet flowers.*

–Lucretius (99 B.C.–55 B.C.)
Ancient Roman poet and philosopher

Garden Design

Public and private gardens and parks provide us with places to relax and enjoy ourselves. Many people enjoy gardening as a hobby, and residential gardens have changed over the years in a way similar to how fashions change, since new cultivars are introduced and others fall out of favor. Although the design of a garden is a matter of personal taste, a few guidelines can be followed. The success of your garden design depends mainly on how well your chosen plants fit with your soil and climate. What do you think are important factors to consider when choosing plants for the garden?

PLANNING YOUR GARDEN

First, you need to determine your hardiness zone by consulting the United States National Arboretum site listed in the Further Reading section. This will narrow your choice of perennial plants to those that can survive the winter in your area. Plants that are native to the region where they are cultivated are already adapted to the soil and climate and require less work than exotic plants. If you have a passion for an exotic plant that has requirements completely different from what your climate and soil have to offer, it will be much more of a challenge to grow.

You can get a general idea of the types of plants that are native to your area by determining the natural ecosystem of the region. Do you live high in the mountains, in the desert, in the plains of the Midwest, along the coast, in the cold North or subtropical Deep South? Cultivars from similar ecosystems in other parts of the world may thrive in your garden.

Next, choose the location of the garden. The placement of the garden has to consider the angle of the sun, which differs in summer and winter and affects light quality. Make a diagram of the area you intend to cultivate and note the number of hours of sunshine it receives. Shadows cast from buildings, trees, walls, and other structures change over the course of the day and from season to season, so it helps to take some time to make observations before you decide on your location and design. Determine whether the site receives full sun, part sun, part shade, or shade, and further narrow down your list of plants to those that will thrive under those light conditions. Also, if you want to plant a lawn you must distinguish between turf grasses that thrive in sun versus those that like shade.

Finally, determine the type of soil in your chosen site by sending samples to a local soil-testing laboratory and telling them the types of plants you would like to grow. They will recommend whether you need to amend your soil pH or add fertilizers or compost, and in what amounts. Also make sure that if your plants require supplemental water, you are near enough to a source that you can easily water them when necessary. Most plants, including those that tolerate drought, require supplemental water until they have established a strong root system—this could take more than a year.

You can get more ideas for plants to try in your garden by reading garden magazines, taking trips to local garden centers, or by looking through seed catalogs and talking to your neighbors. Seed catalogs offer the greatest selection, but if you want more immediate results you need to purchase bedding plants. You may also want to incorporate woody ornamentals and a lawn into your landscape. Most gardens are a work in progress and may take years to complete.

Once you have a list of the particular plants suitable for your site, you must group them together in some sort of an artistic arrangement by color, shape, and size and make sure they are timed to bloom so that the garden has year-round appeal. Usually six of each type of flowering plant are grouped together to get a more vivid display of color. The color and shape of both the foliage and flowers are considered. A mix of plants with different photoperiods blooms at different times and provides a longer display than plants that bloom all at once. Annuals bloom from spring through fall and are often used in combination with perennials that only bloom for a month or two each season.

Figure 7.1 Small ponds with water lilies or other aquatic plants are popular features of formal gardens. The garden above is located in Ravello, Italy.

Fragrant flowers are chosen to perfume the air. A garden that is used at night may have plants with white flowers and silver foliage that reflects the moonlight.

Formal garden designs include geometric patterns created with carefully pruned woody ornamentals and plants with colorful and sweetly scented blossoms, and may have works of art such as statues or frescoes incorporated into the design. There can be fountains to cool the temperature in the heat of the day and benches on which to sit and enjoy the tranquility of the garden. Small ponds or artificially created water gardens are cultivated to produce water lilies and other water-loving plants (Figure 7.1).

Landscaping may also be required to add plants back to soil that has been disturbed by construction or other human activity. Plants that grow quickly from seed and form fibrous roots are often used to stabilize steep banks that are prone to erosion. You can increase wildlife habitat with the creation of a wildflower meadow or create privacy with trees, thickets, or hedges, which will also provide food and shelter for wildlife and act as windbreaks to slow the wind and create microclimates (Figure 7.2).

Figure 7.2 Deryl James from Trees Unlimited in Saratoga, Wyoming, stands next to a windbreak planted on a residential building site.

Plants such as philodendrons are often used in public and private indoor spaces to add visual interest and to purify the air. In these cases, the plants are usually chosen for their distinctive foliage and low maintenance and are planted in decorative containers. These plants are usually tropical plants with attractive large leaves that do not require full sun.

BED PREPARATION AND PLANTING

Once the garden is designed, it needs to be planted but the beds must be prepared first. There are numerous ways to prepare a garden bed. Most of them involve tilling the soil with a shovel. Soil that is loosened to a depth of 1 foot (0.3 meter) will accommodate most garden plants. Larger garden areas may be tilled with a gas-powered rototiller, which can be rented for the day. The beds should be narrow enough that you can comfortably reach across and work with plants. The length of the beds can vary according to available space and the amount of effort you are able to put into the garden, but is usually no longer than 50 feet (15 m). Paths between beds need to be large enough to accommodate a wheelbarrow or garden cart.

Raised beds are often used because they provide easier access to the crops and require less digging to prepare (Figure 7.3). They may be enclosed with wooden boards, or stone or concrete blocks. Pressure-treated wood is avoided because it can leach toxic chemicals into your soil. Raised beds are on average about 8 inches (20.3 centimeters) high. Some root crops may require a depth of 1 foot (0.3 m) and some crops, such as lettuce, can be 6 inches (15.2 cm) high. The beds can be filled with homemade compost and soil from your yard, or you can purchase soil and compost from a nursery.

It is also important to know the history of land use where you want to plant your garden. If the former owners have used high amounts of pesticides, it may affect your ability to grow plants. Also, certain soils should not be disturbed to create a

Figure 7.3 Raised beds can be made from wood, stone, or concrete. Stone was used for raised beds at the Villa Ruffolo in Ravello, Italy (TOP), while wood was the material of choice for raised beds in this private garden in Swanton, Vermont (BOTTOM).

garden, as they have a more important purpose, such as habitat for rare plants or animals and wetlands. Poor soil may be difficult to bring into good tilth; you may have better success with containers.

Container growing is an option that has become increasingly popular. Crops grown in containers require less preparation and maintenance than those grown in garden beds, and they can be moved. Two additional benefits to container horticulture are fewer problems with microbial diseases and weeds. Containers can be made of clay, plastic, wood, or metal. Plastic holds water better than the other materials and is lighter. Wood helps keep the soil temperature from wide fluctuations. Metal may get very hot. Clay dries out fairly quickly and can break more easily than the others but is good for use with plants, such as cactus and succulents, that prefer to be kept on the dry side. Containers should have holes at the bottom to allow for drainage or they can be modified so that they retain water away from the roots, in a bottom reservoir under an absorbent material. These are the so-called self-watering containers and are especially useful in arid climates. When space is an issue, you can create a vertical garden with plants that like to climb, by placing containers near walls or by using a trellis (Figure 7.4).

You can create microclimates in your garden to modify your climate and increase your options for the types of plants you can grow. For example, you may be able to grow cold-sensitive plants against a south-facing wall that holds heat if you cover them with a straw mulch in the winter. Plants that are sensitive to cold temperatures can also be protected with plastic or glass enclosures or row covers. Windbreaks are used to slow the wind before it gets to the garden. Open-weave fences with some spaces, such as a lattice or woven branches, break up the wind very well. Solid structures tend to generate wind currents. Living fences can be created with small trees or hedges;

Figure 7.4 A small lemon grove and flowers in planters create a lush garden in a small space.

Figure 7.5 The use of a retaining wall to create level garden beds is widely used on the steep Amalfi coast of Italy, as demonstrated by this garden at the Villa Scarpariello.

steep slopes can be modified with terraces. Terraces create level garden beds on steep slopes through the use of retaining walls (Figure 7.5).

If you live in an urban area and do not have access to a balcony or rooftop, you may be able to join a community garden in your neighborhood. Community gardens are often created in vacant lots. You may volunteer your time to help clean up the lot in exchange for a plot in which to grow your garden. You may also try to grow plants indoors in containers either on a sunny windowsill or with the aid of supplemental lights. The ancient horticultural art of **bonsai** creates miniature landscapes in small containers.

SUMMARY

A good garden design considers the location of the garden and the amount of sunlight, the limitations of climate, soil, and available space, and balances them with the time and money that can be devoted to planting and maintenance. The next, and last, chapter provides information on the specialized professions within the discipline of horticulture.

8 Horticultural Professions

A journey of a thousand miles must begin with a single step.
–Lao-tzu (c. 604 B.C.–c. 531 B.C.)
Chinese philosopher

Horticultural Professions

Some folks garden to grow good food, others grow gardens for the flowers. Some delight in a green, freshly cut lawn or an early spring blooming orchid in a sunny living-room window. Some like the fact that the garden adds value to their real estate. There are even those that turn their passion for gardening into a profession. There are quite a few options for the horticulturist, as described below.

A degree in horticulture can provide additional opportunities. Horticulture degrees are offered at land-grant colleges (Figure 8.1). Every state has a land-grant college and they are usually part of large state universities. Land-grant colleges were started in the late 1800s by a congressional act sponsored by Justin Morrill from Vermont, as public institutions to teach agriculture. You can find the land-grant college campus locations online at the National Association of State Universities and Land-Grant Colleges Web site listed in the Further Reading section.

Land-grant colleges offer courses that expose you to all the facets of horticulture. Some areas of specialty include horticultural therapy, business management, floriculture, vegetable production, fruit production, woody ornamentals, turf, landscape architecture, greenhouse management, seed production, and plant breeding.

Horticulture therapists work with patients in gardens at hospitals, community centers, retirement homes, and schools. Business managers can work in nurseries, greenhouses, and horticultural supply companies. Floriculturists can work in greenhouse or field production of cut flowers and ornamental houseplants, as wholesale distributors, or in florist shops as flower arrangers. Fruit and vegetable production offers employment in production, management, postharvest distribution, and wholesale and retail of plants, seeds, and produce.

Landscape architects serve diverse clients and may design gardens for homeowners, corporations, commercial sites, and

Figure 8.1 A horticultural student plucks spent flowers of *Pelargonium* geraniums at Colorado State University's trial flower garden.

public spaces. Gardeners and landscape maintenance companies are employed by the same clientele. Turf specialists can be employed by the owners of golf courses and athletic fields. Plant breeders and researchers can find employment in the laboratory or greenhouse, or in field research for botanical gardens, universities, or with private companies. Those with advanced degrees in horticulture also teach at colleges and universities.

The cooperative extension service is a nationwide network associated with universities in every state. The cooperative extension offers free classes that certify you as a master

Plant Collectors

One of the more adventurous horticultural professions is that of the plant collector. The earliest recorded expedition was by the Egyptian queen Hatusu (Hatshepsut) in approximately 1495 B.C. The sought-after plants in this trip were those that produced frankincense and myrrh, used in Egypt for embalming, incense, cosmetics, and medicine. The live trees were transported from the Land of Punt (coastal Somalia, Eastern Sudan, Eritrea) via the Red Sea, Gulf of Suez, and the Nile River.

Botanical gardens were created for scholarly purposes. The earliest botanical gardens were in European universities established in the 1500s and 1600s in France, Italy, the Netherlands, and Germany. In the 1700s, the use of a **terrarium** made possible the survival of many more of the plants collected on explorations, by transportation under glass on long ship voyages. Seeds or cuttings were taken from rare and endangered plants.

The USDA initiated approximately 45 plant collection expeditions in the twentieth century. The USDA horticulturists traveled around the world to collect specimens. One of the USDA horticulturists was Dr. Edward Corbett, a professor of horticulture at the University of Connecticut. Dr. Corbett, while employed as a research horticulturist for the USDA in 1966, accompanied Dr. Richard W. Lighty, a geneticist, on an expedition to South Korea to collect specimens of woody ornamentals. Together they endured travel over rough terrain, long boat rides, typhoons, dysentery, and sunstroke but managed to collect approximately 500 specimens, some of which still grow in Longwood Gardens, a 1,050-acre horticultural display garden in Pennsylvania. Such a trip would be more difficult today because of increased security and government regulations that seek to limit the entry of nonnative plant species into the United States.

gardener in exchange for volunteer service with the extension. You can find more information about this program at the American Horticultural Society Web site listed at the back of the book.

You can also find out about current trends in horticulture from periodicals such as *Horticulture Magazine* or *Organic Garden*, which may be in your local public library. Field trips to botanical gardens, university greenhouses, local nurseries, and garden tours are other ways you can further explore the realm of horticulture.

Glossary

Adventitious roots Structures evolved to absorb water and minerals, which form on a stem cutting.

Agronomy A branch of agricultural science that concentrates on cereal grains and crops to feed domesticated animals.

Algal growth Green aquatic organisms that generate carbohydrates through photosynthesis. Their growth in nonpolluted water is limited by a lack of nutrients such as phosphate or nitrate.

Alkaloids Secondary constituents produced by plants that are usually poisonous but may have medicinal applications.

Aquifers Porous geological features that retain water.

Archaeological data Skeletal remains, fossils, and evidence of human activity found in the soil.

Best management practices Methods used to limit the amount of chemical fertilizer or pesticides applied to the soil, which includes integrated pest management and knowledge of plant physiology to apply fertilizers only in the amounts needed by a plant at a particular time.

Biological control The intentional release or cultivation of beneficial insects or microbes that attack pests that feed on plants.

Bonsai The art of growing miniature or dwarf plants by restriction of root and shoot growth. Plants are grown in shallow containers and the roots and shoots are mechanically pruned or bound.

Breeding The deliberate creation of a new subspecies (variety or cultivar) of plant.

Carotinoid Red or yellow pigments found in leaves, which function as accessory pigments to chlorophyll during photosynthesis.

Chlorophyll Green pigments found in the chloroplast, which function in photosynthesis by absorbing blue or red wavelengths of light.

Chloroplasts Plant organelles that contain chlorophyll pigments and are the site of photosynthesis.

Classification The grouping and naming of plants based on morphological or genetic attributes.

Climate The prevailing weather conditions based on average rainfall and temperature.

Companion plants Plants that provide a beneficial service to the garden by protecting other plants from insect infestation, microbial infection, or nutrient deficiency.

Compost Material produced from a process that degrades plant and animal matter into soil organic matter called humus; a term used interchangeably with humus to describe soil organic matter.

Cotyledon First leaf or leaves that appear after germination.

Crop rotation A method of growing specific plants in a different bed or field in successive years; it reduces the ability of insect pests and microbial disease organisms to increase in population by changing the location of their host plants.

Cultivate To till the soil to prepare for seeding or transplanting, for weed control, and to loosen soil that has developed a crust.

Cultivars Subspecies bred by man.

Cuttings Pieces of stem, leaf, or root taken from a plant and used to propagate a new plant.

Deciduous A plant that drops its leaves in the winter and goes into a dormant state.

Domesticated An adjective to describe an animal or plant which has been bred for food and has genetic and morphological differences from its closest wild relative that render it more useful to humans.

Dormant A state of rest in which a plant is not actively growing.

Double cropping The practice of growing two different plants in the same plot during a single growing season. Usually one is smaller than the other and matures earlier in the season. The second is taller and matures later in the season.

Erosion Loss of soil due to the action of wind or water.

Essential oils Volatile substances, such as alkaloids and terpenes, that are produced by some plants and used for perfume and for medicinal and culinary purposes after a distillation process.

Evergreen A plant that retains its leaves in the winter.

Flats Rectangular trays made of plastic or wood that are used to germinate seeds.

Glossary

Floriculture A branch of horticulture dedicated to the study of ornamental plants.

Forage A vegetable food for animals.

Genetic engineering Human-mediated insertion of foreign genes into a plant chromosome.

Genetically modified organisms (GMO) Plants or microbes with a human-mediated insertion of a foreign gene.

Geologic Relating to the subsurface beneath the soil, which consists mainly of rock.

Grafting Combining a scion from one plant with the rootstock of another.

Groves Collections of citrus, olive, or coconut trees.

Half-hardy A plant able to survive a mild frost, but not a hard frost, without injury.

Hardy A plant that is able to survive a hard frost without injury.

Herbicides Chemicals used to kill a plant.

Horticulture A branch of agricultural science that focuses on plants grown in a garden, with specialties in olericulture, pomology, floriculture, and landscape plants.

Humus The fertile residue of plants and animal matter left after natural decomposition or the compost process. It is also called compost or organic matter.

Hydroponics A method to grow plants without soil in water supplemented with nutrients or in a special potting media.

Indore method A type of composting developed by Sir Howard Albert in India that places specific ratios of organic materials such as vegetable matter and animal manures into large piles called windrows, which generate high heat during decomposition.

Infestation A large population of destructive insects gathered on a plant.

Integrated pest management (IPM) A decision-making process used to manage organisms that are harmful to plants that is based on a fundamental knowledge of ecology.

Invasive A plant that crowds out native plants in the ecosystem.

Irrigation The application of water to crops from a well or surface water body, such as a pond or river, to supplement low rainfall.

Land-grant colleges State-run public institutions that teach agriculture, initiated in the late 1800s through a congressional act that granted federal land to each state, which was sold to fund the establishment of the colleges.

Landscape horticulture A branch of horticulture that specializes in the use of woody ornamentals and turf.

Last average frost date A date in the late spring after which it is generally safe to plant tender annuals. It is calculated based on the historical average date of the last spring frost for a particular region.

Leaching The movement of water and soluble chemicals downward through the soil as a result of gravity.

Leguminosae A family of plants characterized by a dehiscent dry fruit (legume) formed from a single carpel that splits down the side; many are capable of nitrogen fixation with symbiotic microbes.

Mica An aluminosilicate mineral that separates into transparent thin sheets or flakes.

Microbes Organisms too small to be seen without the aid of a microscope, which include bacteria, fungi, algae, protists, nematodes, and viruses.

Monocropping Planting a large plot or field with the same plant variety or cultivar.

Morphological Physical characteristics used to describe the external form of a plant.

Morphology The external form of an organism.

Neolithic revolution A period of human history that occurred roughly 10,000 years ago during the latest period of the Stone Age and resulted in detectable numbers of artifacts related to agriculture and its widespread practice.

Nitrates A form of nitrogen fertilizer that is very soluble in water.

Nitrogen fixation Ability of specific microbes to convert atmospheric nitrogen to a soluble soil mineral.

Nodules Roundish, knobby structures found on the roots of legumes

Glossary

involved in nitrogen fixation. They are generated by an interaction between the plant and its associated nitrogen-fixing microbe. Nodules limit the entry of oxygen, which can inhibit the reaction.

Nurseries Commercial operations dedicated to growing and selling woody ornamentals.

Olericulture Branch of horticulture dedicated to the study or production of vegetables.

Orchards Collections of fruit trees, such as apples, pears, and peaches.

Organic matter The result of decomposed plant, insect, and animal matter plus the microbes that decompose it. Compost and humus are terms that are sometimes used interchangeably.

Ovary Female reproductive organ that contains ovules (eggs).

Parthenocarpy The development of fruit without fertilization or seeds.

Pathogens A microbe that is capable of causing disease.

Percolation The movement of water down through the soil to the groundwater as a result of gravity.

Petals Flower structures that may lure pollinators through bright colors or fragrance.

Pheromone A chemical substance released by an organism to attract members of the opposite sex.

Phloem Vascular tissue that transports sugar from the leaves to the rest of the plant.

Phosphate A form of phosphorous fertilizer that is insoluble in water but may enter into streams and lakes attached to soil particles that run off during an erosion event.

Photoperiod The amount of time per day that a plant is exposed to light.

Photosynthesis Plant physiological process that occurs in chloroplasts in parenchyma cells and uses energy from sunlight to combine carbon dioxide and water into sugar.

Physiology A study of the physical and chemical processes involved in plant development and growth.

Plantlets Cloned plants growing on gelatinous media.

Pollination The transfer of pollen from the male reproductive organ of an angiosperm plant to the stigma of a female reproductive organ.

Pomology A branch of horticulture that specializes in the study or growth of fruit.

Precipitation Rain and snow.

Propagation The generation of new plants.

Pruning Removal of dead branches or sometimes live branches of woody plants to promote health or to change the shape.

Resins Amorphous, flammable substances formed in plant secretions that can be extracted in organic solvents.

Run off Soil and water from heavy rainfall or irrigation events that move in drainage patterns towards surface water bodies.

Seed gene banks Collections of seeds used to preserve genetic diversity in domesticated crops.

Sepals The individual units of the outer layer of a flower bud. They may be green or can closely resemble petals, depending upon the species.

Soil pores Spaces between individual soil particles and between aggregates of soil particles.

Somatic embryo A plant embryo generated by tissue culture from a somatic (nonreproductive) cell that is capable of growth to a mature plant.

Spores Small, sometimes cylindrical reproductive structures produced by seedless plants and some microbes that remain dormant until favorable conditions, such as moisture, cause them to germinate.

Stamen Part of the male reproductive organ in flowering plants, comprised of anthers with pollen suspended on a filament.

Stolons Modified stems that act as asexual reproductive structures produced by some plants such as strawberries. Stolons form adventitious roots and shoots when they come in contact with the soil, thus generating a new plant.

Taxonomy A system of classification concerned with the heredity and evolutionary relationships of organisms.

Tender Describes an annual plant that is injured by a mild frost.

Terraces Level garden beds on a steep slope created through the use of retaining walls.

Glossary

Terrarium An enclosed glass chamber used to grow moisture-loving plants.

Tillage To loosen the soil and turn it.

Tilth Capability of a soil to support growth of garden plants; refers to the texture and structure.

Topiary Artistic shaping of woody ornamental plants by careful pruning.

Transpiration The loss of water as a vapor from leaves to the atmosphere.

Transplant To move a plant from one location to another.

Trichome hairs Small filamentous structures found on leaves or stems that may be soft or rough and may contain glands that produce resin or essential oil.

Turf Grass that is mowed to form a lawn, golf course, or athletic field.

Turgor pressure Pressure generated from water that enters the vacuole in a plant cell; contributes to growth and keeps the plant from wilting.

Variegated A leaf with a mottled appearance.

Vascular system Tissue that moves fluids through a plant.

Vermiculite A lightweight, highly water-absorbent material created from mica by exposure to high heat.

Vernalization Period of cold temperature required by certain plants before they will produce flowers.

Very tender Describes an annual plant that can be killed by a mild frost.

Viable Able to grow and reproduce.

Viticulture The study or process of growing grapes.

Weeds Plants that compete with crops or garden plants for water and nutrients.

Woody ornamentals Plants with a lateral meristem that generates secondary growth and results in an increase in the diameter of the stem. Trees and shrubs are examples.

Xeric A climate characterized by cool, wet winters and hot, dry summers. The term is also applied to plants that thrive in this type of climate.

Xylem Vascular tissue that transports water from the roots up to other parts of the plant.

Yield The harvested portion of a crop measured in units or by weight.

Anisko, Tomasz. *Plant Exploration for Longwood Gardens.* Portland, Ore.: Timber Press, 2006.

Ashworth, Suzanne. *Seed to Seed.* Decorah, Iowa: Seed Savers Exchange, 1991.

Bailey, L.H. *How Plants Get Their Names.* Mineola, N.Y.: Dover Publications, 1963.

Bradley, Fern Marshall and Barbara W. Ellis. *Rodale's All-New Encyclopedia of Organic Gardening: The Indispensable Resource for Every Gardener.* Emmaus, Pa.: Rodale Press, 1992.

Brickell, Christopher and Judith D. Zuk. *The American Horticultural Society A–Z Encyclopedia of Garden Plants.* New York: DK Publishing, 1996.

Campbell, Neil A. *Biology* 4th ed. Menlo Park, Calif.: Benjamin/Cummings Publishing Company, 1996.

Childe, Gordon V. *The Dawn of European Civilization,* 6th ed. New York: Alfred A. Knopf, Inc., 1958.

de Candolle, Alphonse. *Origin of Cultivated Plants,* Reprint of 2nd ed. (1886). New York: Hafner Publishing Company, 1959.

Ellis, Barbara W. and Fern Marshall Bradley. *Organic Gardener's Handbook of Natural Insect and Disease Control: A Complete Problem-Solving Guide to Keeping Your Garden and Yard Healthy without Chemicals.* Emmaus, Pa.: Rodale Press, 1992.

Fedoroff, Nina V. and Nancy Marie Brown. *Mendel in the Kitchen: A Scientist's View of Genetically Modified Foods.* Washington, D.C.: Joseph Henry Press, 1999.

Fernald, M.L. *Gray's Manual of Botany: A Handbook of the Flowering Plants and Ferns of the Central and Northeastern States and Adjacent Canada,* 8th ed. Illustrated. New York: D. Van Nostrand Company, 1970.

Flint, Mary Louise and Steve H. Dreistadt. *Natural Enemies Handbook: The Illustrated Guide to Biological Pest Control.* Berkeley, Calif.: University of California Press, 1998.

Friederici, Peter. "Earthwormed over." *Audubon* March 2004: 28.

Fuller, Andrew S. *The Small Fruit Culturist.* New York: Judd Orange and Company, 1867.

Hancock, James F. *Plant Evolution and the Origin of Crop Species,* 2nd ed. Cambridge: CABI Publishing, 2004.

Harlan, Jack R. *Crops & Man.* Madison, Wisc.: American Society of Agronomy, Crop Science Society of America, 1975.

Bibliography

Harlan, Jack R. *The Living Fields: Our Agricultural Heritage.* Cambridge: Cambridge University Press, 1995.

Janik, Jules. *Horticultural Science*, 4th ed. New York: W.H. Freeman and Company, 1986.

Kohnke, Helmut and D.P. Franzmeier. *Soil Science Simplified*, 4th ed. Prospect Heights, Ill.: Waveland Press, 1995.

Martin, Deborah L. and Grace Gershuny. *Rodale Book of Composting.* Emmaus, Pa: Rodale Press, 1992.

Mithen, Steven. *After the Ice: A Global Human History, 20,000–5000 B.C. .* London, UK: Weidenfeld and Nicolson, 2003.

Nelson, Paul V. *Greenhouse Operations and Management*, 4th ed. Englewood Cliffs, N.J.: Prentice-Hall, 1991.

Poincelot, Raymond P. *Sustainable Horticulture: Today and Tomorrow.* Upper Saddle River, N.J.: Pearson Education, 2004.

Pollen, Michael. "Exploring the Safety and Ethics of Genetically Engineered Foods," in *Genetically Engineered Foods,* Nancy Harris, ed. Farmington, Mass.: Greenhaven Press, 2004: 13–29.

Rabalais, N.N., R.E. Turner, and D. Scavia. "Beyond Science into Policy: Gulf of Mexico Hypoxia and the Mississippi River." *BioScience* 52 (2002): 129–142.

Raven, Peter, Ray F. Evert, and Helena Curtis. *Biology of Plants,* 2nd ed. New York: Worth Publishers, 1976.

Smith, Miranda and the Northeast Organic Farming Association and Cooperative Extension. *The Real Dirt: Farmers Tell About Organic and Low Input Practices in the Northeas*t. Burlington, Vt.: Northeast Region Sustainable Agriculture Research and Education (SARE), 1994.

Storl, Wolf D. *Culture and Horticulture: A Philosophy of Gardening.* Wyoming, R.I.: Bio-Dynamic Literature, 1979.

Swiader, John M., George W. Ware, and J.P. McCollum. *Producing Vegetable Crops,* 4th ed. Danville, Ill.: Interstate Publishers, 1992.

Taiz, Lincoln and Eduardo Zeiger. *Plant Physiology.* Redwood City, Calif.: The Benjamin/Cummings Publishing Company, 1991.

Valpuesta, Victoriano. *Fruit and Vegetable Biotechnology.* Boca Raton, Fla.: CRC Press, 2002.

Verzole, Roberto. "Genetically Engineered Foods Have Health Risks," in *Genetically Engineered Foods,* Nancy Harris, ed. Farmington, Mass.: Greenhaven Press, 2004: 38–42.

von Linne, Carl. *Linnaeus' Philosophica Botanica* translated by Stephen Freer. New York: Oxford University Press, 2003. (First published in Latin in 1751 in Stockholm.)

Ward, Bobby J. *The Plant Hunter's Garden: The New Explorers and Their Discoveries.* Portland, Ore.: Timber Press, 2004.

Zohary, Daniel and Maria Hopf. *Domestication of Plants in the Old World: The Origin and Spread of Cultivated Plants in West Asia, Europe and the Nile Valley,* 3rd ed. New York: Oxford University Press, 2000.

Further Reading

Appelhof, Mary. *Worms Eat My Garbage: How to Set Up and Maintain a Worm Composting System.* Kalamazoo, Mich.: Flower Press, 1982.

Bix, Cynthia, Philip Edinger, and the Editors of Sunset Books. *Arranging Flowers from Your Garden.* Menlo Park, Calif.: Sunset Publishing Corporation, 2002.

Coleman, Eliot. *The New Organic Grower: A Master's Manual of Tools and Techniques for the Home and Market Gardener.* White River Junction, Vt.: Chelsea Green Publishing Company, 1995.

Doty, Walter L. *All About Vegetables.* San Ramon, Calif.: Ortho Books (Monsanto Company), 1990.

Jeavons, John. *How to Grow More Vegetables.* Berkeley, Calif.: Ten Speed Press, 1995.

Kowalchik, Claire and William H. Hylton, Eds. *Rodale's Illustrated Encyclopedia of Herbs.* Emmaus, Pa.: Rodale Press, 1998.

Ondra, Nancy J. and Saxon Holt. *Grasses: Versatile Partners for Uncommon Garden Design.* North Adams, Mass.: Storey Books, 2002.

Riotte, Louise. *Carrots Love Tomatoes: Secrets of Companion Planting for Successful Gardening.* Pownal, Vt.: Storey Communications, 1975.

Stickland, Sue. *Greenhouses: Natural Vegetables, Fruit, and Flowers All the Year Round.* Coventry, UK: The Henry Doubleday Research Association, 1993.

Wilson, Gilbert L. *Buffalo Bird Woman's Garden: Agriculture of the Hidatsa Indians.* St. Paul, Minn.: Minnesota Historical Society Press, 1987.

Web Sites

American Horticultural Society

www.ahs.org/master_gardeners/index.htm

This Web site has a link to the horticultural cooperative extension Master Gardening Program and links to various publications.

Environmental Protection Agency

http://www.epa.gov

This site has information on pesticides and legislation for the conservation of water and soil.

National Association of State Universities and Land-Grant Colleges

www.nasulgc.org/campus.htm

Land-grant college Web sites have links to the horticultural cooperative extension for your state, which provide fact sheets online and can recommend a soil testing lab.

Natural Resources Conservation Services

http://www.nrcs.usda.gov

This site has a link where teachers and students can find out about conservation of soil and water with Backyard Conservation Tip sheets. There is also a plant database.

USDA Web site

http://www.usda.gov

This site has links for information on organic certification and commercial horticultural crops.

United States National Arboretum

http://www.usna.usda.gov

This site has an interactive USDA Plant Hardiness Zone Map, virtual tours and plant galleries of woody ornamentals, a list of state trees and flowers plus horticultural links with information on pest management.

The following sites offer virtual tours, image galleries, and links to garden and horticultural information on plants from different ecosystems.

Brooklyn Botanic Garden (http://www.bbg.org) is in New York City.

Denver Botanic Garden (http://www.botanicgardens.org) is in Colorado.

Desert Botanic Garden (http://www.dbg.org) is in Arizona.

Hawaii Tropical Botanical Garden (http://www.htbg.com) is in Hawaii.

Longwood Gardens (www.longwoodgardens.org) is in Pennsylvania.

Missouri Botanic Garden (http://www.mobot.org) is in St. Louis.

Royal Botanic Gardens: Kew (http://www.rbgkew.org.uk) is in England.

The Berry Botanic Garden (http://www.berrybot.org) is in Oregon.

United States Botanic Garden (http://www.usbg.gov) is in Washington, D.C.

Index

Index

light, 48–51, 86
Lighty, Richard W., 106
lilies, 20, 23
lime, 54–55
Linnaeus, Carolus, 26, 27
loams, 51
location, selection of, 92–93
Low Input Sustainable Agriculture
    (LISA) program, 15

macronutrients, 52
maintenance, overview of, 74–77
media, 36
meristem cells, 40
methyl bromide, 67
microbes, 10, 13–14, 64–66, 70, 85
microclimates, 98
micronutrients, 52–53
minerals, 8–10, 51, 53–54
moisture. *See* water
Mollison, Bill, 14
monocotyledons, 19, 20, 22, 23
monocropping, 10, 67–68, 73, 81–83
mulching, 67, 75
mutations, breeding and, 41
mycorrhizal fungi, 66

naming of plants, 24–29
night length, 50
nitrates, 12
nitrogen, 55, 56, 66
nitrogen fixation, 22, 66, 70
nodules, 22
nutrients, 36, 52–53, 55, 70, 74

olericulture, 5
orchards, 5
orchids, 39
organic gardening, 55–56, 74–75
organic matter, 10, 52
organic produce, 12–15
ovaries, 18–19, 25
oxygen, 56, 70

parenchyma cells, 39–40
parthenocarpic fruits, 25, 42
pathogens, 65, 66–67
perennial plants, 22, 75–76, 92
permaculture, 14
pesticide drift, 81
pesticides, 10, 14–15, 33, 42–43, 81, 85
pests, 69–74
pH, 53–55, 56, 74–75
pheromone traps, 85–86
phloem, 19
phosphorus, 55, 56
photoperiod, 50–51
photosynthesis, 19, 48, 49
phyllosphere, 69–73
pigments, 24, 50
pollination, 7, 34–35, 41, 69
pomology, 5
ponds, 94
post-harvest handling, 89
potassium, 54–56
potatoes, 41, 81, 82
predators, 73
pretreatments, 33–34
propagation, 32–36, 36–39, 39–44
pruning, 7, 77
Pseudomonas, 67

rain. *See* water
raised beds, 96, 97
resins, 22
retaining walls, 100
rhizomes, 38
rhizosphere, 64–69
ripening, 88–89
rock phosphate, 55
Rodale, J.I., 14
roots, 38, 41, 57–59
rot, gray, 75, 76
rototillers, 96

salts, 54
sandy soils, 51

Picture Credits

Gail M. Lang has studied plants for more than 20 years. She holds a Ph.D. in environmental microbiology from Colorado State University, an M.S. in genetics, and a B.S. in agronomy from the University of Connecticut. She has professional experience in the commercial greenhouse and botanical garden; has conducted research in the field, laboratory, and greenhouse; and was an inspector for certification of organic farms. She currently gardens in the foothills of the Rocky Mountains and researches plant biodiversity at an avian preserve.